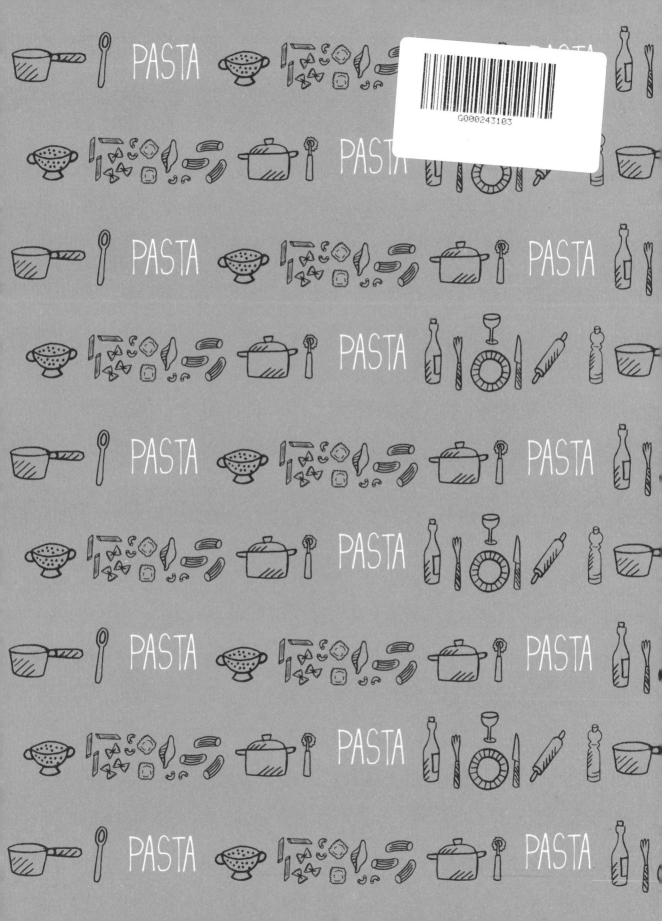

Recipes and food styling by Valéry Drouet
Photos by Pierre-Louis Viel

VALÉRY DROUET & PIERRE-LOUIS VIEL

PASTA

[FRESH, SIMPLE, AND DELICIOUS]

h.f.ullmann

FOREWORD

The simplest things are always the best!

Discover, or re-discover, pasta! Dried or fresh, baked, in a salad, or stuffed—pasta in its many variations is all about entertaining large groups of friends or family around the dinner table. Great times, when the really important thing is sharing!

Why not try making your own ravioli, lasagne, or cannelloni? It is so easy, as well as extremely satisfying! This book will provide you with all the instructions you need to make wonderful and delicious pasta recipes in a range of colors. If you are pushed for time, it goes without saying that all the recipes using fresh pasta can equally well be adapted to dried versions.

Whether cooking with meat, fish, seafood, cheese, vegetables, or herbs, you should never skimp on quality. Our delicious pasta recipes will bring out the best in these ingredients, are great fun to make and fuss-free.

Just choose a nice bottle of wine if you like, get ready to enjoy your labor of love, and Buon appetito!

Valéry Drouet

CONTENTS

PASTA SECCA (Dried pasta)

PASTA FRESCA (Fresh pasta)

RAVIOLI

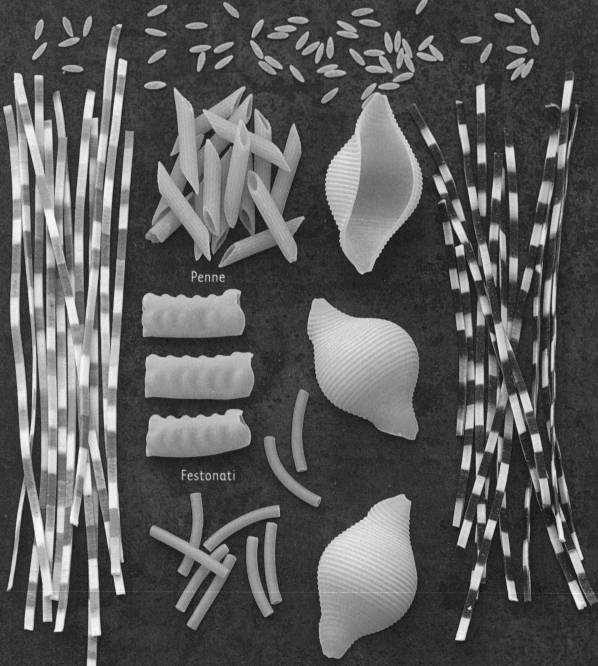

DRIED

Multi-colored pasta

Puntalette

Penne

Festonati

Macaroni

Conchiglioni

Zebra pasta

PASTA

Fusilli

Cannelloni rigate

Pasta shells

Fettuccine

Linguine

DRIED PASTA

Tips and adVice

There are dozens of different types of pasta available, especially those made by artisanal or specialist pasta producers. You will be able to find them in supermarkets and Italian delicatessens.

If you use ready-made pasta, go for the ones made with durum wheat and fresh eggs. Excellent dried pasta brands, as well as an incredible selection of pasta in different colors, are now available from an increasing number of delicatessens and supermarkets.

Use small pasta—shells, puntalette, baby macaroni, or trofie twists, for instance—to make dishes like *pastasotto* (risotto made with pasta instead of rice).

Medium-size pasta like penne, fusilli, or dondolini (to name but a few) are suitable for many recipes, including cold pasta salads.

Spaghetti, linguine, fettuccine, and tagliardi are the perfect pasta types for one-dish meals.

And of course there is a wide range of pasta suitable for fillings—cannelloni, large shells, and lasagne—which are ideal if you have a crowd to feed. When cooking dried pasta, simply follow the instructions on the packet, as the cooking time varies according to the size, type, and even the brand of pasta.

Cook the pasta uncovered in a large pan of boiling salted water. The rule is the same as for fresh pasta: 1 quart (1 liter) of water and 2 teaspoons (12 g) of salt per 3½ ounces (100 g) of pasta. When cooking spaghetti, use a pan with high sides (you can buy special spaghetti pans) so that it can be plunged whole into the water, or alternatively you can break the pasta in half before submerging it in the boiling water.

Finally, in terms of quantities of dried or fresh pasta, allow 3½ ounces (100 g) per person approximately, or slightly more if it is a single dish meal (taking into account any accompanying side dishes).

FRESH

With beetroot

With squid ink

With parsley

With turmeric and
sesame seeds

PASTA

FARFALLE

1

2

3

4

ORECCHIETTE

1

2

3

4

RAVIOLI

TORTELLI

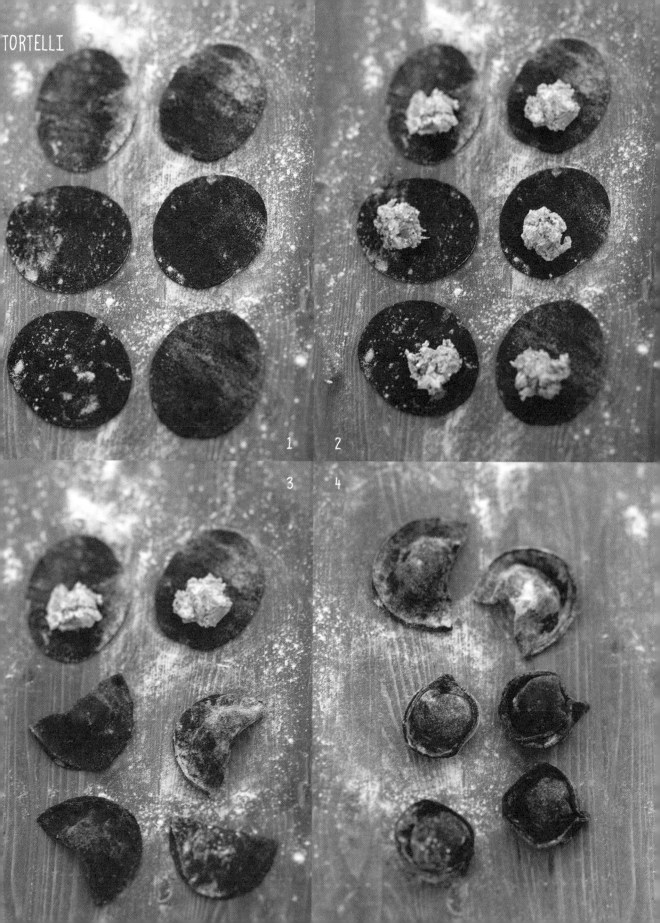

1   2

3   4

FRESH PASTA

Try making your own fresh pasta—a process that will allow you to enjoy eating pasta in all sorts of shapes, sizes, and flavors, giving your imagination free rein to create the food you love. You can even color the dough in different ways (using squid ink or beetroot juice), flavor it with herbs and spices, and play around with shapes and lengths if you like.

Two tips before you begin:

- always use extra-fresh eggs when making the dough for pasta shapes or ravioli;

- dust your pasta machine (rolling mill), work surface, and hands liberally with flour when working the dough to make farfalle, orecchiette, ravioli, and other tortelli. Make sure the dough does not become too dry between the two stages of making pasta or ravioli, as it soon turns brittle and difficult to handle.

RECIPE FOR FRESH PASTA

Makes generous 1 lb (500 g) pasta

- 2 2/3 cups (400 g) all-purpose flour
- 4 large eggs
- 1/3 cup (80 ml) olive oil
- 2 tsp (12 g) salt

⟫ Put the flour in the bowl of a food processor with a flat beater attachment. Add the eggs, salt, and olive oil. Whizz the processor for a few minutes at a low speed setting until you have a smooth dough that comes away cleanly from the sides of the bowl. If it still sticks, add a little more flour; if it is too dry, add a small amount of olive oil or cold water.

⟫ Shape the dough into a ball and cover in plastic wrap. Leave to rest for at least 2 hours in the refrigerator.

⟫ Roll out the dough in small batches, preferably using a pasta roller (or a rolling pin until it is very thin, about 1 mm thick), then cut it into the shape required: tagliatelle, farfalle, or ravioli for example (see photos on pages 16–19).

⟫ Dry the pasta for 2 to 3 hours on a small pasta drying rack or use a wooden handle. Store the fresh pasta in the refrigerator for up to 4–5 hours.

⟫ If you prolong the drying time (12–24 hours at room temperature) you will have dried pasta which can be stored in an airtight jar.

⟫ For darker colored dough, use 3 whole eggs and 2 yolks (the same quantity of salt and olive oil). Remember, depending on the quality of the eggs, your dough will be more or less yellow naturally: if you get the chance to use fresh farm eggs, you will notice the difference!

HOW TO COOK PASTA

》 The cooking time for fresh pasta ranges from 3 to 6/7 minutes, depending on the thickness. Put it into a large pan of boiling salted water (1 quart/1 liter of water and 2 teaspoons/12 g of salt per 3½ ounces/100 g of pasta).

》 Three to four minutes is plenty for fresh ravioli. However, make sure the water is simmering (if it is boiling too hard, your ravioli or tortellini could burst and lose their filling).

》 The important thing to remember when cooking all pasta types is to cook them *al dente*—that is, still slightly firm to the bite (when overcooked they become soft).

》 Once the pasta is cooked, drain it quickly and do not rinse. Serve immediately with olive oil, butter, or sauce, or sauté it in a frying pan along with other ingredients.

》 Always keep some of the pasta cooking water to add to the sauce if it is a bit too thick, or if you want to eat them plain. All you need to do is melt some butter in a ladle-full of cooking water to dress the pasta—served with some freshly grated Parmesan cheese, it is simply delicious!

》 If your pasta is to be eaten cold in a salad or at a later time, however, rinse it in a sieve under cold water and mix in a drizzle of oil to prevent it from sticking. Similarly, after the pasta has been cooked, if you have left it too long before using it hot and it has stuck to the sieve, rinse briefly in hot water or drizzle some oil through it.

ADDING FLAVOR AND COLOR TO YOUR PASTA DOUGH

》 For pink pasta

Add 2–2½ ounces (50–70 g) extra flour and scant ½ –²/₃ cup (100–150 ml) beetroot juice.

》 For black pasta

Add 2 tablespoons (30 ml) of squid ink (available in sachets or small jars from the fresh seafood counter of supermarkets, or from your retailer).

》 For green pasta

Chop 1 large bunch of curly parsley. Wrap the chopped parsley in a clean piece of muslin and squeeze it until you have 5–7 tablespoons (80–100 ml) of juice. Mix this juice into the dough (add some flour if it is too sticky).

》 For yellow pasta

Mix 1 tablespoon of turmeric powder with 3 tablespoons of cold water and work it through the dough. If you like, you can also add 2 tablespoons of black sesame seeds, poppy seeds, or mustard seeds.

DRIED PASTA

PREPARATION: **15 minutes**

COOKING THE PASTA:

see packet instructions

INGREDIENTS

Serves 6

- 1¼ lb (600 g spaghetti)
- 1¾ lb (750 g) cherry tomatoes
- 1 large bunch basil
- 2 cloves garlic
- ²/₃ cup (150 ml) olive oil
- salt, ground pepper

HOT 'N' COLD SPAGHETTI WITH CHERRY TOMATOES

≫ Remove the stalks from the basil. Peel the garlic cloves.

≫ Put the basil and garlic in a food grinder (or blender). Add the olive oil and season with salt and pepper. Whizz for 3–4 minutes until the basil oil is nice and smooth.

≫ Wash and halve the tomatoes (or quarter them, depending on size). Put them in a bowl. Add the basil oil and mix well.

≫ Cook the spaghetti in a large pan in plenty of boiling salted water (follow the cooking time on the packet). Drain the pasta.

≫ Mix the spaghetti with the tomatoes and oil in the bowl. Spoon into shallow bowls and serve immediately.

TIP

Alternatively, you can sear the cherry tomatoes for 2 minutes in a large frying pan with 3 tablespoons of olive oil. Deglaze the pan briefly with 3 tablespoons of balsamic vinegar and stir through the pasta.

BAKED MACARONI AND CHEESE WEDGES

PREPARATION: 15 minutes

COOKING THE PASTA:
see packet instructions

OVEN COOKING TIME:
25–30 minutes

INGREDIENTS

Serves 6

- generous 1 lb (500 g) small elbow
  macaroni
- 12 processed cheese wedges
- 4 ham slices, fairly thick
- 1 $^2/_3$ cups (400 ml) light cream
- salt, ground pepper

》 Cook the pasta in a large pan in plenty of boiling salted water (follow the cooking time on the packet). Drain in a sieve and rinse under cold water.

》 Pre-heat the oven to 180 °C (350 °F).

》 Put 6 of the cheese wedges in a pan along with the cream and season with salt and pepper. Bring to a boil on medium heat and stir well with a spatula until the mixture is nice and smooth.

》 Chop up the ham slices into small pieces.

》 Mix the pasta in a bowl with the cheese sauce and ham.

》 Divide the mixture between individual fondue pots (or a large gratin dish). Sprinkle the remaining cheese wedges, finely diced, on top.

》 Bake in the oven for 25–30 minutes. Serve immediately.

RAINBOW PASTA WITH PEAS, BROAD BEANS, AND THYME

PREPARATION: **30 minutes**
COOKING THE PASTA:
see packet instructions

INGREDIENTS

Serves 6

- 1¼ lb (600 g) multi-color pasta (from delicatessens or Italian grocers)
- 1¼ lb (600 g) fresh peas, shelled
- 1¼ lb (600 g) broad beans, shelled
- 2 cloves garlic
- 1 bunch fresh thyme
- 1 ⅔ cups (400 ml) good vegetable stock
- ⅓ cup (80 g) butter
- salt, ground pepper

> Cook the peas and broad beans separately for 5 minutes in boiling salted water. Drain and rinse under cold water.

> Remove the broad bean skins. Peel the garlic cloves.

> Pour the vegetable stock into a pan. Add the whole garlic cloves, thyme, and salt and pepper. Boil vigorously for 10 minutes to reduce the liquid by one third. Add the chopped cold butter, and boil rapidly again for 6–8 minutes.

> Remove the thyme sprigs and garlic, then whizz the stock with a hand blender.

> Put the peas and broad beans in the stock and keep it hot.

> Cook the pasta in a large pan of boiling salted water (follow the cooking time on the packet).

> Drain the pasta and put into the pan along with the vegetables and sauce. Mix well and serve immediately.

Replace the multi-color pasta with fresh home-made pasta, with added color. This recipe is a real rainbow of colors!

Spaghetti carbonara with qua eggs

PREPARATION: **30 minutes**
COOKING THE PASTA:
see packet instructions

INGREDIENTS

Serves 6

- 1¼ lb (600 g) spaghetti
- 18 quail eggs
- 1¾ lb (750 g) bacon slices,
  $^1/_5$ inch (5 mm) thick
- ¾ cup (80 g) Parmesan, grated
- 2 cups (500 ml) light cream
- 2 tbsp sunflower oil
- salt, ground pepper

> Prepare the quail eggs by separating the whites from the yolks. Keep the yolks in their shells in the refrigerator and discard the whites.

> Cut the bacon slices into small lardons (chunks). Put them in a pan, cover with cold water, and bring to a boil for 30 seconds. Drain and then brown them in a frying pan in the oil for 2 minutes on medium heat. Blot up the oil with paper towels.

> In a pan, boil the cream for 8—10 minutes on medium heat, adding salt and pepper to taste. Add the Parmesan and boil for 30 seconds. Whizz the sauce with a hand blender. Add the bacon bits and keep it hot.

> Cook the spaghetti in a large pan in plenty of boiling salted water (follow the cooking time on the packet). Drain the pasta.

> Spoon the bacon sauce onto the plates. Put the spaghetti on top, forming three little nests in each dish. Place a quail egg yolk in the top of each nest. Serve immediately.

Vermicelli with crispy celeriac, Parma ham, and Earl Grey

PREPARATION: **50 minutes**

COOKING THE PASTA:
8–10 minutes

INGREDIENTS

Serves 6

- generous 1 lb (500 g) vermicelli
  (angel hair pasta)
- 14 oz (400 g) celeriac
- 12 thin slices Parma ham
- $^1/_3$ cup (50 g) all-purpose flour
- 1¼ quarts (1¼ liters) chicken stock
- 1 Earl Grey teabag
- 1 quart (1 liter) vegetable oil for
  frying
- salt, ground pepper

> In a pan, add salt and pepper to the chicken stock and bring to a boil for 2 minutes. Switch off the heat. Add the teabag and leave to infuse for 10 minutes. Remove the teabag.

> Cut the ham into thin strips.

> Peel the celeriac and cut into julienne strips (ideally using a mandolin, or else a knife).

> Put the flour into a bowl. Add the celeriac strips and mix well so they are evenly coated.

> Heat the vegetable oil in a pan for deep-frying. Using a wire mesh skimmer, dip the ham slices in for a few seconds until they are nice and crispy. Drain on paper towels. Then deep-fry the celeriac strips for 2–3 minutes. Drain on paper towels.

> Bring the tea-infused stock back to a boil for 2 minutes. Turn off the heat. Add the vermicelli, cover the pan, and allow them to swell for 8–10 minutes.

> Pour the vermicelli soup into shallow dishes. Arrange the crispy celeriac and fried ham on top. Serve immediately.

PENNE WITH ARTICHOKES, PANCETTA, AND LEMON THYME

PREPARATION: **40 minutes**

COOKING THE PASTA:

see packet instructions

INGREDIENTS

Serves 6

- 1¼ lb (600 g) penne
- 15 small purple artichokes
- 18 slices pancetta
- 3 shallots
- 1 bunch lemon thyme
- juice of 1 lemon
- generous ¾ cup (200 ml) white wine
- ⅓ cup (80 g) butter
- 7 tbsp (100 ml) olive oil
- salt, ground pepper

> Remove the tough outer leaves of the artichokes. Pare round the base with a small knife, cut them in half and place in a bowl of water containing the lemon juice.

> Peel and chop the shallots. Sweat them in a large frying pan with 5 tablespoons of olive oil for 3 minutes on medium heat.

> Add the artichokes and cook for 2 minutes. Pour in the white wine and ⅔ cup (150 ml) of water. Season with salt and pepper. Cover the pan with wax paper and cook for 15 minutes on medium heat.

> Transfer the artichokes into a dish. Reduce the cooking juices for 5 minutes on high heat. Add the chopped butter and thyme leaves. Boil for a further 5–7 minutes to thicken the sauce. Strain it into a bowl with high sides and then whizz with a hand blender until smooth. Pour it back into the frying pan along with the artichokes and keep hot.

> Cook the pasta in a large pan in plenty of boiling salted water (follow the cooking time on the packet).

> Meanwhile, chop the pancetta and sauté for 2 minutes in a frying pan with the rest of the oil. Lift the pancetta out onto a plate lined with paper towel.

> Drain the pasta and divide between the plates. Spoon the artichokes and pancetta on top. Pour the sauce over and serve immediately.

FUSILLI WITH GREEN ASPARAGUS AND CHEESE

PREPARATION: **20 minutes**
COOKING THE PASTA:
see packet instructions

INGREDIENTS

Serves 6

- 1¼ lb (600 g) fusilli
- 1¼ lb (600 g) small green asparagus
- 9 oz (250 g) cheese (Monterey Jack)
- 5½ oz (150 g) arugula (rocket)
- 3 pinches saffron strands
- 2 vegetable bouillon cubes
- 3 tbsp balsamic vinegar
- 7 tbsp (100 ml) olive oil
- salt, ground pepper

》 Peel the asparagus and tie them in a bunch. Bring a pan of salted water containing 1 bouillon cube to a boil. Immerse the asparagus, cook for 5–6 minutes, and then drain.

》 Cook the pasta in plenty of boiling salted water with the other bouillon cube and the saffron (follow the cooking time on the packet).

》 Meanwhile, brown the asparagus on a lightly oiled grill or frying pan for 4–5 minutes.

》 Drain the pasta and put it in a bowl. Add three-quarters of the olive oil, some balsamic vinegar, and season with salt and pepper.

》 Grate the cheese. Dress the arugula with the remaining oil, vinegar, and salt and pepper to taste.

》 Divide the pasta and asparagus between the plates. Scatter a few arugula leaves on top and sprinkle with grated cheese. Serve immediately.

TIP

Add a crunchy dimension to the recipe by making some cheesy tuiles. Place little mounds of grated cheese on a non-stick baking tray and bake in a pre-heated oven (180 °C/350 °F) for 6-8 minutes. Lift them off the tray with a plastic spatula and leave to cool.

CLASSIC MACARONI CHEESE

PREPARATION: **20 minutes**
+ overnight soak

COOKING THE PASTA
see packet instructions

OVEN COOKING TIME
20–25 minutes

INGREDIENTS

Serves 6

- 1¼ lb (600 g) elbow macaroni
- 1¼ cups (140 g) grated Gruyère
- scant 2 cups (90 g) breadcrumbs
- 1 quart (1 liter) milk
- 4 tbsp (60 g) butter + 2 tsp (10 g)
  to grease the dish
- 1¼ cups (300 ml) light cream
- salt, ground pepper

> The night before, cook the pasta in a large pan in plenty of boiling salted water (follow the cooking time on the packet). Drain in a sieve and rinse under cold water. Put the pasta in a container, cover in milk, and then seal with plastic wrap.

> On the day, pre-heat the oven to 180 °C (350 °F).

> Drain the macaroni, reserving 7 tablespoons of the milk. Mix the pasta in a bowl with the reserved milk, cream, ¾ cup (80 g) o grated cheese, and some salt and pepper.

> Grease a large gratin dish with butter and line with 1 ounce (30 g) of the breadcrumbs. Put the macaroni in the dish and sprinkle on the remaining cheese and breadcrumbs. Dot the mixture all over with finely diced butter.

》 Bake for 20—25 minutes until the top is golden and crispy. Brown under the oven broiler if it is still too pale.

》 Serve the gratin as a main dish, or to accompany a nice roast chicken, or a red or white meat. A feast for kids and adults alike!

FUSILLI PAESANI WITH CHICKEN AND CREAMY PARMESAN

PREPARATION: **20 minutes**

COOKING THE PASTA:

see packet instructions

INGREDIENTS

Serves 6

- 1¼ lb (600 g) fusilli paesani
- 1½ lb (700 g) cooked roast chicken meat
- 1 $^1/_3$ cups (150 g) Parmesan, freshly grated
- 2 onions
- 1 small bunch flat-leaf parsley
- 1 chicken bouillon (stock) cube
- 1 $^2/_3$ cups (400 ml) light cream
- 3 tbsp olive oil
- salt, ground pepper

> Remove the chicken skin and chop the meat into small pieces.

> Peel and slice the onions. In a large frying pan, brown the onions in the olive oil for 8–10 minutes on medium heat until a light golden color.

> Add the chopped chicken to the pan; season with salt and pepper, mixing well. Brown the mixture for 2 minutes on medium heat and leave in the frying pan.

> In a pan, boil the cream for 2 minutes along with half of the Parmesan and a pinch of salt and pepper. Keep the sauce hot (in a double boiler).

> Wash and chop the parsley.

> Cook the pasta in plenty of boiling salted water containing the bouillon cube (follow the cooking time on the packet).

> Drain the pasta and combine with the chicken mixture in the frying pan. Add the Parmesan cream and mix it through.

> Divide the chicken pasta between the plates. Sprinkle with parsley and serve immediately with the remaining Parmesan in a side dish.

CANNELLONI WITH VEAL AND SPINACH

PREPARATION: 30 minutes
OVEN COOKING TIME:
40–45 minutes

INGREDIENTS

Serves 6

- 24 cannelloni tubes
- 1¾ lb (800 g) veal fillets (medallions), ground
- 14 oz (400 g) whole spinach, cooked and frozen
- 1¾ cups (200 g) Comté cheese, grated
- 1 red onion
- 2 cloves garlic
- 3 ⅓ cups (800 ml) passata or purée
- 3 tbsp olive oil
- salt, ground pepper

≫ Defrost the spinach leaves in a sieve and then chop them up.

≫ Pre-heat the oven to 160 °C (320 °F).

≫ Peel and chop the onion and garlic. In a large frying pan, brown the onion and garlic in the olive oil for 3 minutes on medium heat. Add the ground veal and cook for 6–8 minutes on high heat, stirring continuously.

≫ Add the chopped spinach and ⅔ cup (150 ml) of passata. Season with salt and pepper. Stir all the ingredients together well and chill.

≫ Heat the remaining passata in a pan with a small amount of water to thin it slightly.

≫ Fill the uncooked cannelloni tubes with the spinach filling, using your fingers.

≫ Pour some of the passata into a large gratin dish. Arrange the cannelloni on top, packing them tightly together. Cover with the rest of the passata and sprinkle with the grated cheese.

≫ Bake in the oven for 40–45 minutes. Brown the surface for 5 minutes under the oven broiler. Serve immediately.

Replace the veal with well-browned herb sausagemeat. When in season, use fresh spinach and stir the cooking liquid into the passata.

TROFIE PASTASOTTO WITH CRISPY HAM

PREPARATION: 15 minutes
COOKING THE PASTA:
15 minutes approx.

INGREDIENTS

Serves 6

- 1¼ lb (600 g) trofie (small, thin pasta twists from Liguria)
- 12 slices dry-cured ham, not too thin
- 1 ⅓ cups (150 g) Beaufort cheese or Gruyère, grated
- 1 onion
- generous 1¼ quarts (1 ⅓ liters) chicken stock
- generous 2 tbsp thick crème fraîche
- ⅓ cup (80 g) butter
- 2 tbsp olive oil
- salt, ground pepper

> Bring the chicken stock to a boil in a pan.

> Peel and chop the onion. Sweat in an ovenproof casserole dish with 1½ tablespoons (20 g) of butter for 5 minutes on medium heat.

> Add the pasta to the casserole and mix it well through the butter and onion. Cook for 2 minutes. Pour in all of the boiling stock. Season with salt and pepper. Bring to a boil and cook for 12 minutes on medium heat, stirring frequently.

> Meanwhile, cut the ham into thin strips. Brown for 3 minutes in a frying pan with the olive oil and tip onto a plate lined with paper towel.

> Add the crème fraîche to the casserole, mix well, and cook for 3 minutes. Remove from the heat and then add the rest of the cold chopped butter, mixing well to bind it with the pasta and sauce. Add the grated cheese and crispy ham. Serve immediately.

If you cannot source trofie pasta, use Savoy crozets (small, flat pasta squares) or just some small macaroni.

DONDOLINI SALAD WITH GRILLED PEPPERS AND FETA

PREPARATION: **40 minutes**

COOKING THE PASTA:
see packet instructions

INGREDIENTS

Serves 6

- 1¼ lb (600 g) dondolini (large spirals: from Italian delis)
- 2 green bell peppers
- 2 red bell peppers
- 2 yellow bell peppers
- 1 lb (450 g) feta cheese
- 2 cloves garlic
- 20 basil leaves
- 3 tbsp sherry vinegar
- 7 tbsp (100 ml) olive oil
- salt, ground pepper

> Peel and de-seed the peppers; cut them into julienne strips.

> Peel and chop the garlic. Gently chop the basil.

> In a frying pan, stir-fry the pepper strips in 3 tablespoons of olive oil for 1–2 minutes on high heat. Add the chopped garlic, salt, and pepper. Cook for 2 minutes, stirring all the time. Turn off the heat, add the vinegar, remaining olive oil, and the basil. Mix well and leave to cool.

≫ Cook the pasta in a large pan in plenty of boiling salted water (follow the cooking time on the packet). Drain in a sieve and rinse briefly under cold water.

≫ Cut the feta into small cubes. Put the pasta into a large bowl. Add the feta and the oil and pepper mixture from the frying pan. Carefully fold all the ingredients together.

≫ Serve the pasta salad at room temperature or chill for 2 hours before eating.

GNOCCHI WITH NEAPOLITAN SAUCE

PREPARATION: **40 minutes**
COOKING THE PASTA:
see packet instructions

INGREDIENTS

Serves 6

- 1¼ lb (600 g) gnocchi (large pasta shells)
- 18 thin slices Parma ham
- 5 medium size ripe tomatoes
- 2 shallots
- 2 cloves garlic
- 1 bunch fresh thyme
- 1 tbsp tomato purée
- 1 vegetable bouillon (stock) cube
- 3 tbsp olive oil
- salt, ground pepper

≫ Blanch the tomatoes in a pan of boiling water for 20 seconds and then rinse them under cold water. Skin, remove the seeds, and chop the tomatoes roughly.

≫ Peel and chop the garlic and shallots. Brown the shallots in a pan with the olive oil for 3 minutes on medium heat. Add the chopped tomatoes, tomato purée, and salt and pepper to taste. Cook for 3 minutes and then add 3¼ cups (750 ml) of water. Add the bouillon cube and thyme. Cook for 20–25 minutes on medium heat.

≫ Meanwhile, pre-heat the oven to 180 °C (350 °F).

≫ Spread the ham slices on a baking tray lined with wax paper. Bake for 6–8 minutes to dry them out. Allow to cool and then whizz them in a food processor for 2 minutes until they are like coarse breadcrumbs.

≫ Remove the thyme sprigs from the pan. Whizz the tomatoes with a hand blender until the consistency of fairly thick passata. Keep hot.

≫ Cook the pasta in a large pan in plenty of boiling salted water (follow the cooking time on the packet).

≫ Drain the pasta and stir into the hot sauce. Add a few twists of ground pepper. Serve immediately with a side dish of Parma ham crumbs.

FUSILLI WITH SMOKED HADDOCK AND CHIVES

PREPARATION: **30 minutes**

COOKING THE PASTA:
see packet instructions

INGREDIENTS

Serves 6

- 1¼ lb (600 g) fusilli
- 1¾ lb (750 g) smoked haddock
- 1 large bunch chives
- 1¼ cups (300 ml) fish stock
- 3¼ cups (750 ml) milk
- $^1/_3$ cup (80 g) butter
- salt, ground pepper

≫ Heat the milk in a pan.

≫ Remove the skin from the smoked haddock and cut it into large chunks. Poach for 3 minutes in the milk, simmering gently. Turn off the heat and leave the fish in the milk.

≫ In a pan, boil the fish stock rapidly for 5–8 minutes. Add the cold chopped butter, salt, and pepper. Simmer for another 5 minutes to reduce.

≫ Meanwhile, chop the chives.

≫ Whizz the sauce with a hand blender. Add the chives and mix well. Keep the sauce hot in a double boiler.

≫ Cook the pasta in a large pan in plenty of boiling salted water (follow the cooking time on the packet).

≫ Drain the smoked haddock and flake it onto a plate.

≫ Drain the pasta and pour into a pan. Add the hot sauce, haddock, and a few twists of ground pepper. Mix all the ingredients together carefully and serve immediately in shallow dishes.

PREPARATION: **20 minutes**

COOKING THE PASTA:
see packet instructions

FRYING TIME:
4—5 minutes

INGREDIENTS

Serves 6 (makes approx. 12 cakes)

- 14 oz (400 g) small macaroni
- 5½ oz (160 g) Beaufort cheese (or Gruyère)
- 5¼ oz (150 g) soft white cheese
- 3 egg yolks
- 7 tbsp (60 g) all-purpose flour
- 2 tbsp (30 g) butter
- 3 tbsp sunflower oil
- salt, ground pepper

Cheesy pasta cakes

> Cook the pasta in a large pan in plenty of boiling salted water (follow the cooking time on the packet). Drain in a sieve and rinse with cold water.

> Grate the cheese.

> In a bowl, combine the soft cheese with the egg yolks, flour, and a pinch of salt and pepper. Add the pasta and grated cheese.

> Shape the mixture into 12 balls with the palms of your hands and gently flatten them.

> Heat the oil and butter in a large frying pan. When it begins to sizzle, put the pasta cakes into the pan and brown for 4—5 minutes on each side on medium heat, moving them around carefully—do them in batches.

> Drain the pasta cakes on paper towels and serve immediately—delicious with meat or poultry, and kids love them!

VEAL AND HERB STUFFED SHELLS

PREPARATION: **50 minutes**

COOKING THE PASTA:
see packet instructions

OVEN COOKING TIME:
25–30 minutes

INGREDIENTS

Serves 6

- 1¼–1½ lb (600–700 g) conchiglioni
- 1¾ lb (800 g) ground veal
- generous 1 cup (120 g) grated Parmesan
- 1 large white onion
- 2 shallots
- 1 clove garlic
- 1 bunch flat-leaf parsley
- 1 small bunch chervil
- 1 bunch chives
- 3 sprigs tarragon
- 2½ cups (600 ml) passata or tomato purée
- 5 tbsp olive oil
- salt, ground pepper

≫ Cook the pasta in a pan in plenty of boiling salted water for approximately 3–4 minutes. Drain in a sieve and rinse under cold water. Drizzle 2 tablespoons of olive oil through the shells to prevent them from sticking.

≫ Peel and chop the onion, shallots, and garlic. Brown the onion in a pan with the rest of the olive oil for 5 minutes on medium heat. Add the ground veal and sear on high heat for 5–6 minutes, stirring all the time. Season with salt and pepper. Stir in 7 tablespoons (100 ml) of passata and cook for another 5 minutes.

≫ Meanwhile, wash and chop the herbs. Stir the herbs into the meat once it is cooked.

≫ Pre-heat the oven to 180 °C (350 °F).

≫ Heat the remaining passata in a pan, adding a little water to thin it slightly.

≫ Stuff the pasta shells with the herb and meat mixture. Place in a large ovenproof dish. Pour the passata around the shells and sprinkle with grated cheese. Bake for 25–30 minutes. Serve immediately.

Shrimp parcels with balsamic glaze

PREPARATION: 30 minutes

COOKING THE PASTA:

see packet instructions

FRYING TIME:

1 minute

INGREDIENTS

Serves 6

- 11 oz (300 g) spaghetti
- 30 fairly large pink shrimp
- scant 1 cup (250 ml) passata or tomato purée
- scant 1 cup (250 ml) balsamic vinegar
- 1 quart (1 liter) vegetable oil for deep-frying
- 2 tbsp (25 g) superfine sugar
- salt, ground pepper

> Cook the pasta in plenty of boiling salted water (follow the cooking time on the packet). Drain in a sieve and rinse briefly under cold water. Leave to drain in the sieve without adding any oil, so they stick together slightly.

> In a pan, reduce the balsamic vinegar and sugar for approximately 10 minutes until it reaches a syrupy consistency. Add the passata and season with salt and pepper. Cook for 8–10 minutes on medium heat. Keep the sauce hot (in a double boiler).

> Remove the shrimp shells. Insert a wooden skewer through each shrimp then carefully roll some spaghetti around each one, pressing lightly to make them stick together.

> When you are almost ready to serve, heat the frying oil. Deep-fry the shrimp in the very hot oil for just one minute, holding the skewers with your fingers. Drain on paper towels.

> Season the fried shrimp with salt and pepper. Serve immediately with the tomato and balsamic glaze.

STIR-FRY SPAGHETTI AND BEEF TERIYAKI

PREPARATION: **40 minutes**
+ 2 hours for marinade

COOKING THE PASTA:
see packet instructions

INGREDIENTS

Serves 6

- generous 1 lb (500 g) spaghetti
- 1¼ lb (600 g) beef tenderloin or rump
- 7 oz (200 g) oyster mushrooms
- 11 oz (300 g) green beans
- 3 cloves garlic
- 1 tsp freshly chopped chili
- 1 tsp chili powder
- 7 tbsp (100 ml) teriyaki sauce
- 3 tbsp fish sauce (nuoc-mam)
- 3 tbsp sunflower oil
- salt, ground pepper

≫ Cut the meat into thin strips.

≫ Peel and chop the garlic. In a bowl, stir the garlic with the chopped chili, chili powder, fish sauce, teriyaki sauce, a pinch of salt, and some pepper.

≫ Add the meat strips and coat them thoroughly with the marinade, mixing well. Cover with plastic wrap and refrigerate for 2 hours.

≫ Top and tail the green beans and cook for 10 minutes in boiling salted water. Drain and rinse under cold water.

≫ Cook the pasta in a large pan in plenty of boiling salted water (follow the cooking time on the packet). Drain in a sieve, and rinse briefly under cold water.

≫ Carefully wipe the oyster mushrooms and chop finely. Fry them in a pan in the oil for 6–8 minutes on medium heat.

≫ Drain the marinade off the meat (reserving it) and then sear the meat for 4–5 minutes in a frying pan together with the mushrooms, stirring all the time, on high heat.

≫ Add the green beans, spaghetti, and marinade. Re-heat for 3–4 minutes on high heat, coating the pasta with the sauce. Serve immediately.

PREPARATION: **50 minutes**

COOKING THE PASTA:

see packet instructions

INGREDIENTS

Serves 6

- 1¼ lb (600 g) festonati
- 7 oz (200 g) sardines in olive oil
- 1 head of garlic
- 1 bunch basil
- 6 tbsp (50 g) pine nuts
- 7 tbsp (100 ml) olive oil
- salt, ground pepper

FESTONATI WITH SARDINE PESTO AND BAKED GARLIC

≫ Pre-heat the oven to 180 °C (350 °F).

≫ Wrap the whole head of garlic in a sheet of aluminum foil. Bake in the oven for 35–40 minutes. Take it out of the oven and leave to cool.

≫ Squeeze out the soft garlic pulp from each clove. Put the garlic pulp in a food processor (or blender) with the basil leaves, pine nuts, olive oil, and drained sardines. Whizz until the sardine pesto reaches a smooth consistency.

≫ Cook the pasta in plenty of boiling salted water (follow the cooking time given on the packet).

≫ Drain the pasta and put it in a frying pan. Add the pesto and stir through. Re-heat for 5 minutes on medium heat and serve immediately.

PREPARATION: **30 minutes**

COOKING THE PASTA:
see packet instructions

INGREDIENTS

Serves 6

- 14 oz (400 g) rigatoni
- scant 1¼ cups (300 g) ricotta or soft
  sheep's milk cheese
- 4 oz (120 g) pitted black olives
- scant 1 cup (100 g) grated Parmesan
- 10 basil leaves
- 7 tbsp (100 ml) olive oil
- salt, ground pepper

RIGATONI WITH RICOTTA AND OLIVES

> Cook the pasta in a large pan in plenty of boiling salted water (follow the cooking time on the packet). Drain in a sieve and rinse briefly under cold water.

> Put the olives, basil leaves, and half of the oil in a food grinder. Whizz it all into a paste.

> In a bowl, mix together the olive paste with the ricotta, some pepper, and a pinch of salt.

> Using a pastry bag with a medium nozzle, carefully fill the rigatoni with the mixture. Arrange the rigatoni on a baking tray lined with wax paper.

> Pre-heat the oven broiler to 200 °C (390 °F).

> Drizzle the remaining olive oil over the pasta and sprinkle with Parmesan. Brown it under the broiler for 5–6 minutes. Serve immediately with mixed salad leaves.

PREPARATION: **15 minutes**
COOKING THE PASTA:
12–15 minutes

INGREDIENTS

Serves 6

- 1¼ lb (600 g) fusilli
- 2 oz (60 g) fresh truffle (or a jar)
- 3 tbsp truffle sauce, or a few drops of truffle essence
- 4 oz (120 g) piece of aged Parmesan
- 1½ quarts (1½ liters) rich chicken stock
- 7 tbsp (100 g) butter
- salt, ground pepper

FUSILLI WITH TRUFFLES AND PARMESAN

≫ In a large pan, bring the stock to a boil, adding the truffle sauce and salt and pepper.

≫ Add the pasta and stir with a spatula until it starts to boil again. Cook for 12–15 minutes on medium heat, stirring frequently.

≫ Meanwhile, slice the truffle very finely. Using a vegetable peeler, make large Parmesan shavings.

≫ When the pasta is cooked, turn off the heat, add the cold chopped butter, and stir it in until it has melted (it will thicken the stock slightly).

≫ Spoon the pasta and stock into shallow dishes. Sprinkle with truffle slices and Parmesan shavings. Give a twist of ground pepper and serve immediately.

ZEBRA PASTA WITH LOBSTER AND GARLIC SAUCE

**PREPARATION: 1 hour
+ 2 hours in refrigerator
for the lobster**

**COOKING THE PASTA:
see packet instructions**

INGREDIENTS

Serves 6

- 1¼ lb (600 g) striped linguine
  (from Italian delis)
- 3 lobsters, each weighing approx.
  1¼ lb (600 g)
- 1 carrot
- 1 red chili
- 3 shallots
- 6 cloves garlic
- 1 tbsp tomato purée
- 3 tbsp olive oil + 1 drizzle
- ⅓ cup (80 g) butter

≫ Cook the lobsters in plenty of boiling salted water for 10 minutes. Drain, rinse under cold water, and refrigerate for 2 hours.

≫ Remove all the lobster shells (keep them to one side). Cut the tails into chunks and chill them.

≫ Peel and chop the shallots and carrot. Brown them in a large pan with the olive oil for 3 minutes on medium heat. Add the lobster shells and sear on high heat for 5 minutes. Mix in the tomato purée and cover completely with water. Bring to a boil and cook for 30 minutes on medium heat.

≫ Peel the garlic cloves. De-seed and slice the chili. Strain the seafood stock to remove the lobster shells and vegetables before transferring the liquid stock into a pan with the whole garlic cloves and chili. Boil rapidly on high heat to reduce to approximately 2 cups of liquid. Add the diced butter and boil for a few more minutes to bind the sauce. Strain the sauce to remove the garlic and chili and place them to one side. Whizz with a hand blender until smooth.

≫ Pop the garlic and chili back into the sauce. Add the lobster pieces and keep the sauce hot (in a double boiler).

≫ Cook the pasta in a large pan in plenty of boiling salted water (follow the cooking time on the packet). Drain and drizzle with olive oil.

≫ Spoon the pasta onto the plates and add the pieces of lobster along with the sauce. Serve immediately.

Crispy cannelloni rigate with crab

PREPARATION: **20 minutes**

COOKING THE PASTA:
see packet instructions

FRYING TIME:
6–8 minutes

INGREDIENTS

Serves 6

- 11 oz (300 g) cannelloni rigate
- 7 oz (200 g) crab meat
- 9 oz (250 g) fresh soft goat milk
  cheese
- 1 carrot
- 2 cups (100 g) breadcrumbs
- 2 tbsp (30 g) butter
- 3 tbsp olive oil
- salt, ground pepper

≫ Cook the pasta in a large pan in plenty of boiling salted water (follow the cooking time on the packet). Drain in a sieve and rinse under cold water. Spread the pasta out flat on a baking tray.

≫ Put the breadcrumbs on a plate.

≫ Peel the carrot and dice it finely. Blanch for 3 minutes in a pan of boiling salted water. Drain.

≫ In a bowl, mix together the drained crab meat, goat cheese, and carrot. Season with salt and pepper.

≫ Using a pastry bag, carefully stuff the cannelloni tubes with the mixture. Roll the tubes in breadcrumbs, pressing down gently.

≫ Just before serving, heat the butter and oil in a pan, and brown the cannelloni for 3–4 minutes on each side on medium heat. Serve immediately as a starter or with aperitifs.

You can equally well use large cannelloni tubes. In this case, stuff them whole after cooking and then cut them into sections with a very sharp knife.

PREPARATION: **15 minutes**

COOKING THE PASTA:
12–14 minutes

INGREDIENTS

Serves 6

- 14 oz (400 g) puntalette pasta (see p. 10)
- 1 onion
- ¾ cup (80 g) grated Parmesan
- 7 tbsp (100 ml) white wine
- 3¾ cups (900 ml) chicken stock
- 2½ tbsp (40 g) butter
- 2 tbsp olive oil
- salt, ground pepper

PUNTALETTE *PASTASOTTO*

> Heat the stock in a pan.

> Peel and chop the onion. Brown it gently in a large pan in the olive oil for 5 minutes.

> Add the pasta to the pan and stir well, coating it all over with the onion and oil. Add the wine and bubble it off for 3 minutes on high heat.

> Pour the stock into the pasta in batches, stirring occasionally and waiting for it to be absorbed before adding more. Season with salt and pepper.

> When the pasta is cooked *al dente* (allow 12–14 minutes cooking time), remove the pan from the heat before adding the chopped cold butter and grated Parmesan. Stir in quickly with a spatula. Serve the *pastasotto* immediately in shallow dishes.

FRESH PASTA

SPAGHETTI BOLOGNAISE WITH VEAL

PREPARATION: **45 minutes + 4–5 hours drying time for the dough and spaghetti**

COOKING THE PASTA: **4–5 minutes**

INGREDIENTS

Serves 6

- 2¾ lb (scant 1.2 kg) ground veal fillet
- 1¾ cups (200 g) Gruyère cheese, grated
- 2 carrots
- 1 onion
- 2 sprigs fresh thyme
- 1¼ cups (300 ml) passata or tomato purée
- generous ¾ cup (200 ml) veal or beef stock
- 2½ tbsp (40 g) butter
- 3 tbsp olive oil
- salt, ground pepper

For the dough (makes generous 1 lb/500 g spaghetti)

- 3 cups (400 g) all-purpose flour
- 4 large eggs
- ⅓ cup (80 ml) olive oil
- 2 tsp (12 g) salt

› Make the spaghetti dough as described in the basic recipe for fresh pasta (see p. 20, § 1 and 2).

› When the dough has rested, roll it out on the work surface and make the spaghetti. Leave to dry for 2–3 hours.

› Peel and chop the onion. Peel the carrots and dice them finely. In a casserole dish, brown the onion and carrot in the olive oil for 6–8 minutes on medium heat.

› Add the ground veal and sear for 6–8 minutes on high heat, stirring all the time.

≫ Add the passata and stock. Season with salt and pepper and add the thyme sprigs. Cook for 30 minutes on medium heat.

≫ Just before serving, cook the spaghetti in plenty of boiling salted water for 4–5 minutes. Drain and put the pasta in a bowl. Add the butter and mix well.

≫ Spoon the spaghetti into shallow bowls. Serve immediately with the veal bolognaise and grated cheese.

GREEN LINGUINE WITH GRILLED CHICKEN

PREPARATION: 50 minutes + 4–5 hours drying time for the dough and linguine

COOKING THE PASTA: 6–7 minutes

INGREDIENTS

Serves 6

- 6 chicken breasts
- 3½ oz (100 g) arugula (rocket)
- 3 tbsp (20 g) pine nuts
- ¼ cup (30 g) grated Parmesan
- 10 cloves new season garlic
- ⅔ cup (150 ml) olive oil
- salt, ground pepper

For the dough (makes generous 1 lb/500 g linguine)

- 3 cups (400 g) all-purpose flour
- 4 large eggs
- 1 large bunch curly parsley
- ⅓ cup (80 ml) olive oil
- 2 tsp (12 g) salt

> To make the linguine dough, start by chopping the parsley and squeezing it in a piece of muslin to produce scant 2 teaspoons of liquid. Then make the dough as described in the basic recipe instructions for fresh pasta (see p. 20, § 1 and 2), adding the parsley juice together with the oil.

> When the dough has rested, roll it out on the work surface and make the linguine (strips approximately $1/10$ inch/2–3 mm wide). Leave to dry for 2–3 hours.

> Meanwhile peel the garlic. Cut 7 of the cloves into thin slices. Fry them in a small pan in 2 tablespoons of olive oil for 2–3 minutes. Drain on paper towel.

> Pour the rest of the olive oil into a food grinder (or blender). Add the arugula, the 3 remaining whole garlic cloves, pine nuts, Parmesan, and some salt and pepper. Blend for 2 minutes to make a pesto and set aside.

> In a frying pan, cook the chicken breasts in 2 tablespoons of olive oil for 6–8 minutes on each side on medium heat. Cut the chicken into strips.

> Cook the linguine in plenty of boiling salted water for 6–7 minutes. Drain and mix the pasta in a bowl with half of the pesto.

> Spoon the linguine onto the plates. Add the chicken strips, sprinkle with the garlic slivers, and drizzle with the remaining pesto.

Saffron lasagne with shellfish and lemon thyme

PREPARATION: 45 minutes + 4 hours drying time for the dough and lasagne

COOKING THE PASTA: 4–5 minutes

INGREDIENTS

Serves 6

- 2¼ lb (1 kg) cockles
- 2¼ lb (1 kg) clams
- 2¼ lb (1 kg) mussels
- 24 cooked pink shrimp, shells removed
- 2 shallots, peeled and chopped
- 1 bunch lemon thyme
- 2 pinches saffron threads
- 3 tbsp (30 g) all-purpose flour
- 7 tbsp (100 ml) white wine
- ²/₃ cup (150 ml) light cream
- 2 tbsp (30 g) butter
- salt, ground pepper

For the dough (makes generous 1 lb/500 g lasagne)

- 3 cups (400 g) all-purpose flour
- 4 large eggs
- 3 saffron threads
- ¹/₃ cup (80 ml) olive oil
- 2 tsp (12 g) salt

> To make the lasagne dough, first soak the saffron threads in 1 tablespoon of hot water and then follow the basic recipe instructions for fresh pasta (see p. 20, § 1 and 2), mixing in the saffron together with the oil. When the dough has rested, roll it out on the work surface (not too thinly) and cut it into 18–24 squares measuring 4 inches (10 cm) on each side. Leave to dry for 2 hours.

> Meanwhile, melt the butter in a large casserole dish, add the flour, and stir for 3 minutes on medium heat. Set the roux to one side.

> Wash the shellfish thoroughly. In a large pan, boil the white wine together with the shallots. Add the shellfish and thyme. Cover the pan and cook for 10 minutes on high heat, stirring the mixture halfway through the cooking time. Drain the shellfish (reserving the cooking liquid), leave to cool, then remove all the shells.

> Filter the shellfish cooking juices until you have approximately 1 ²/₃ cups (400 ml) and pour the reserved liquid into the casserole containing the roux. Add the saffron and cook for 4–5 minutes on medium heat, stirring all the time, until the sauce thickens slightly. Add the cream, season with salt and pepper, and cook for 4–5 minutes. Stir the shellfish and shrimp into the sauce, mixing well. Keep it hot.

> Cook the lasagne sheets in plenty of boiling salted water for 4–5 minutes. Drain in a sieve and drizzle through some olive oil. Place 1 lasagne sheet on each plate and spoon some sauce and shellfish on top. Repeat this process 2 or 3 times until all the sauce and shellfish has been divided out, finishing each plate with a lasagne square. Serve immediately.

Saffron farfalle with pork and sage

PREPARATION: **50 minutes + overnight drying for the dough and farfalle**

COOKING THE PASTA:
6–7 minutes

INGREDIENTS

Serves 6

- 2 lb (900 g) pork tenderloin fillet
- 12 sage leaves
- 1¼ cups (300 ml) gravy or veal (or beef) stock
- ⅔ cup (150 ml) white wine
- 3 tbsp olive oil
- 2½ tbsp (40 g) butter
- salt, ground pepper

For the dough (makes generous 1 lb/500 g farfalle)

- 3 cups (400 g) all-purpose flour
- 4 large eggs
- 3 pinches saffron threads
- ⅓ cup (80 ml) olive oil
- 2 tsp (12 g) salt

≫ Make the farfalle dough the night before. Start by soaking the saffron threads in 2 tablespoons of hot water and then make the dough as described in the basic recipe instructions for fresh pasta (see p. 20, § 1 and 2), mixing in the saffron together with the oil.

≫ When the dough has rested, roll it out on the work surface and shape the farfalle (see p. 16). Leave to dry overnight.

≫ The next day, season the pork fillets with salt and pepper on each side. In a frying pan, seal the meat in the olive oil for 6–7 minutes on each side on medium heat. Wrap each fillet in a sheet of aluminum foil. Leave them on a plate to rest for 10–15 minutes. Chop the sage.

≫ Drain the oil from the frying pan and place the pan on a high heat. Deglaze with the white wine and reduce the volume by half. Add the gravy or stock and reduce by one third. Season with salt and pepper, whip in the cold chopped butter, and add the sage. Keep the sauce hot.

≫ Cook the farfalle in plenty of boiling salted water for 6–7 minutes.

≫ Meanwhile slice the pork fillets and transfer them to the frying pan with the sauce.

≫ Drain the pasta and pile onto the plates. Add the meat and sauce. Serve immediately.

PINK PAPPARDELLE WITH SATAY PRAWNS

**PREPARATION: 50 minutes
+ 5 hours drying time for the
dough and pappardelle**

COOKING THE PASTA:
5–6 minutes

INGREDIENTS

Serves 6

- 36 large pink prawns
- 3½ oz (100 g) satay (Asian seasoning mix made with peanuts and chili)
- 1¼ cups (300 ml) fish stock
- 4 tbsp (60 g) butter
- 3 tbsp olive oil
- salt, ground pepper

For the dough (makes generous 1 lb/500 g pappardelle)

- 3 $^1/_3$ cups (450 g) all-purpose flour
- 4 large eggs
- 7–10 tbsp (100–150 ml) beetroot juice
- $^1/_3$ cup (80 ml) olive oil
- 2 tsp (12 g) salt

》Make the pappardelle dough as described in the basic recipe for fresh pasta (see p. 20, § 1 and 2), mixing in the beetroot juice at the end.

》When the dough has rested, roll it out on the work surface and make the pappardelle (strips approximately ¾ inch/2 cm wide). Leave to dry for at least 3 hours.

》Remove the prawn shells, leaving on the heads and tips of the tails. Brown them in a frying pan in the olive oil for 2–3 minutes on high heat. Season with salt and pepper and add the satay mix. Fry for another 2–3 minutes on high heat, coating the prawns well with the satay. Transfer to a baking tray lined with wax paper.

》Return the frying pan to the stove and deglaze with the fish stock. Boil rapidly for 5 minutes to reduce. Whip in the cold chopped butter, check the seasoning, and keep the sauce hot.

》Pre-heat the oven broiler (grill).

》Cook the pappardelle for 5–6 minutes in plenty of boiling salted water.

》Meanwhile, pop the prawns under the broiler for 3–4 minutes.

》Drain the pappardelle, add them to the sauce in the frying pan, and stir through. Spoon the pasta and sauce onto the plates and place the prawns on top. Serve immediately (sprinkle some satay mix around the plates if so desired).

CANNELLONI WITH SWISS CHARD AND GOAT CHEESE

PREPARATION: **45 minutes + 4–5 hours drying time for the dough and cannelloni**

COOKING THE PASTA: **4–5 minutes**

OVEN COOKING TIME: **15 minutes**

INGREDIENTS

Serves 6

- 1½ lb (700 g) Swiss chard
- generous 1 lb (500 g) fresh goat cheese
- 2 shallots, peeled and chopped
- 1 bunch fresh thyme
- 1¼ cups (300 ml) vegetable stock
- 7 tbsp (100 ml) olive oil + a drizzle
- salt, ground pepper

For the dough (makes generous 1 lb/500 g cannelloni)

- 3 cups (400 g) all-purpose flour
- 4 large eggs
- ⅓ cup (80 ml) olive oil
- 2 tsp (12 g) salt

> Make the cannelloni dough as described in the basic recipe instructions for fresh pasta (see p. 20, § 1 and 2). When the dough has rested, roll it out on the work surface (not too thinly) and cut it into 18 rectangles measuring approximately 4 x 5 inches (10–12 cm).

> Leave to dry for 2–3 hours. Meanwhile clean the Swiss chard by removing the tough parts of the leaves and the stringy part of the stalks. Slice the stalks and leaves.

> In a large frying pan, brown the shallots with half the olive oil for 2 minutes on medium heat. Add the chard stalks and leaves, mix well, and cook for 5 minutes. Pour in half the stock and season with salt and pepper. Cook for a further 12–15 minutes on medium heat. Transfer the mixture to a bowl and chill.

> Cook the pasta rectangles in plenty of boiling salted water for 4–5 minutes. Drain, then rinse them under cold water. Drizzle through a little oil to keep them from sticking together. Lay the pasta rectangles out flat on the work surface.

> Pre-heat the oven to 180 °C (350 °F).

> Crumble the goat cheese and mix it into the chard with a fork. Season with salt and pepper. Spread the cheese and chard mixture over one side of the pasta rectangles. Roll them up carefully to form large cannelloni.

> Put the cannelloni in a large gratin dish, sprinkle with thyme, and drizzle with the remaining stock and olive oil. Bake in the oven for 15 minutes. Serve immediately.

CREAMY TAGLIARDI WITH COCKLES

PREPARATION: 1½ hours
+ 4 hours drying time for the dough and tagliardi

COOKING THE PASTA:
3 minutes

INGREDIENTS

Serves 6

- 5½ lb (2.5 kg) cockles
- 1 carrot
- 1 onion
- 1 bunch fresh lemon thyme
- 1 cup (250 ml) white wine
- 8½ tbsp (120 g) butter
- 3 tbsp olive oil
- freshly ground pepper

For the dough (makes generous 1 lb/500 g tagliardi)

- 3 cups (400 g) all-purpose flour
- 4 large eggs
- ⅓ cup (80 ml) olive oil
- 2 tsp (12 g) salt

》Make the tagliardi dough as described in the basic recipe instructions for fresh pasta (see p. 20, § 1 and 2).

》When the dough has rested, roll it out on the work surface in wide strips and cut into small rectangles measuring approximately 3 x 1¼ inches (7 x 3 cm). Leave to dry for 2 hours.

》Meanwhile wash the cockles thoroughly in several changes of water and then drain them.

》Peel and chop the onion. Peel the carrot and dice it finely. In a large pan, brown the onion and carrot together in the oil for 3 minutes on medium heat. Add the cockles, three-quarters of the thyme, the wine, and the pepper. Cover and cook on high heat for 8—10 minutes, stirring once halfway through the cooking time. Leave to cool and then remove the shells.

》Filter the cooking liquid into a pan until you have approximately 2 cups (500 ml). Boil rapidly for 5 minutes, add the cold chopped butter, and some pepper. Boil for a further 6—8 minutes. Whizz the sauce with a hand blender until creamy and keep it hot in the pan.

》When almost ready to serve, cook the tagliardi in plenty of boiling salted water for 3 minutes. Drain and transfer the tagliardi immediately to the simmering sauce. Add the cockles and the rest of the thyme. Re-heat gently for 3 minutes.

》Spoon the pasta and cockles onto the plates and coat with

Tagliatelle with green tea and ginger langoustines

PREPARATION: 40 minutes + 4–5 hours drying time for the dough and tagliatelle

COOKING THE PASTA: 4–5 minutes

INGREDIENTS

Serves 6

- 30 medium size langoustines
- scant 1 tbsp green tea
- generous 1 tbsp (15 g) freshly grated ginger
- 1¼ cups (300 ml) fish stock
- 3 tbsp rice vinegar
- ⅓ cup (80 g) butter
- 3 tbsp olive oil
- salt, ground pepper

For the dough (makes generous 1 lb/500 g tagliatelle)

- 3 cups (400 g) all-purpose flour
- 4 large eggs
- scant 1 tbsp green tea
- ⅓ cup (80 ml) olive oil
- 2 tsp (12 g) salt

> To make the tagliatelle dough, first soak the green tea in a cup containing 2 tablespoons of hot water and then follow the basic recipe instructions for fresh pasta (see p. 20, § 1 and 2), mixing in the green tea (strained) together with the oil.

> When the dough has rested, roll it out on the work surface and cut it into strips measuring approximately ⅕ inch (5 mm) wide. Leave to dry for 2–3 hours.

> Slit the prawns in half lengthways and remove the black vein. Sear them on the flesh side in a frying pan containing the olive oil for 20 seconds. Transfer the prawns to a baking tray lined with wax paper. Season with salt and pepper.

> Pre-heat the oven broiler (grill).

> Deglaze the frying pan with the rice vinegar. Add the ginger, fish stock, and green tea. Boil rapidly for 5 minutes. Add the cold chopped butter and boil for another 5 minutes. Whizz the sauce with a hand blender (or in a food processor). Season with salt and pepper and keep the sauce hot.

> Cook the tagliatelle in plenty of boiling salted water for 4–5 minutes.

> Meanwhile, pop the prawns under the oven broiler for 4–5 minutes.

> Drain the pasta and pile it onto the plates. Place the prawns on top and pour over the sauce. Serve immediately.

LINGUINE WITH MUSTARD SEEDS AND BEEF

PREPARATION: **45 minutes + 6 hours drying time for the dough and linguine**

COOKING THE PASTA: **5–6 minutes**

INGREDIENTS

Serves 6

- 1¾ lb (750 g) rump steak
- 2 bunches pearl onions
- 3 medium tomatoes
- a few arugula (rocket) leaves
- generous 1 tbsp chili powder
- 7 tbsp (100 ml) wine vinegar
- 1/3 cup (80 g) butter
- 3 tbsp sunflower oil
- salt, ground pepper
- generous 3 tbsp (40 g) superfine sugar

For the dough (makes generous 1 lb/500 g linguine)

- 3 cups (400 g) all-purpose flour
- 4 large eggs
- 2 tbsp mustard seeds
- 1/3 cup (80 ml) olive oil
- 2 tsp (12 g) salt

> Make the linguine dough as described in the basic recipe instructions for fresh pasta (see p. 20, § 1 and 2), mixing in the mustard seeds together with the oil.

> When the dough has rested, roll it out on the work surface and make the linguine (strips approximately $1/10$ inch/2–3 mm wide). Leave to dry for 4 hours.

> Meanwhile peel the pearl onions, leaving them whole. In a frying pan, brown the onions on medium heat with 2 tablespoons of the butter. Dust them with the sugar and caramelize for 3 minutes. Pour in the vinegar and 7 tablespoons of water. Season with salt and pepper. Cover the pan with a sheet of wax paper and cook for 15 minutes on medium heat. Keep it hot.

> Cut the beef steak into thin strips and cut the tomatoes into quarters. In a large frying pan, sear the meat strips in the oil on high heat for approximately 2 minutes on each side. Season with the chili powder, add the tomatoes, and cook for 1 minute on high heat. Add salt to taste and keep hot.

> Cook the linguine in plenty of boiling salted water for 5–6 minutes, then drain. Stir the rest of the butter through the linguine in a bowl. Season with salt and pepper.

> Mix together the onions, tomatoes, and beef strips. Spoon the pasta onto the plates. Top with the meat, onion, and tomato mixture. Garnish with the arugula leaves and serve immediately.

TAGLIATELLE WITH BOTTARGA, FENNEL, AND SAFFRON

PREPARATION: **45 minutes + 4–5 hours drying time for the dough and tagliatelle**

COOKING THE PASTA:

20 minutes

INGREDIENTS

Serves 6

- 1¼ lb (700 g) fennel (2 or 3 bulbs)
- 6½ oz (180 g) bottarga (dried and cured roe of tuna or mullet)
- 3 pinches saffron threads
- 2 cups (500 ml) fish stock
- 6 tbsp (90 g) butter
- 3 tbsp olive oil
- salt, ground pepper

For the dough (makes generous 1 lb/500 g tagliatelle)

- 3 cups (400 g) all-purpose flour
- 4 large eggs
- 2 pinches saffron threads
- ¹/₃ cup (80 ml) olive oil
- 2 tsp (12 g) salt

> To make the tagliatelle dough, start by soaking the saffron in a cup containing 1 tablespoon of warm water, then follow the basic recipe instructions for fresh pasta (see p. 20, § 1 and 2), mixing in the saffron together with the oil.

> When the dough has rested, roll it out on the work surface and cut it into strips measuring approximately ¹/₅ inch (5 mm) wide. Leave to dry for 2–3 hours.

> Peel and finely slice the fennel. Brown it in a frying pan with the olive oil for 8–10 minutes on medium heat. Season with salt and pepper. Keep it hot.

> In a pan, boil the fish stock rapidly to reduce it by one third. Add the cold chopped butter and saffron. Mix together well and boil on high heat for 6–8 minutes. Whizz the sauce with a hand blender or processor until smooth and keep it hot (in a double boiler).

> Cook the tagliatelle in plenty of boiling salted water for 6–7 minutes, then drain.

> In a bowl, combine the tagliatelle and fennel. Season with salt and pepper.

> Spoon the fennel pasta onto the plates. Pour on the saffron sauce and sprinkle some bottarga shavings on top. Serve immediately.

Black linguine with squid

PREPARATION: **50 minutes**
+ 4–5 hours drying time for the
dough and linguine

COOKING THE PASTA:
4–6 minutes

INGREDIENTS

Serves 6

- 3¼ lb (generous 1½ kg) baby squid
- 4 tomatoes
- 1 carrot
- 1 celery stalk
- 1 onion
- 4 cloves garlic
- generous 2 tbsp (30–35 ml) squid
  ink
- 1 ²/₃ cups (400 ml) white wine
- 7 tbsp (100 ml) olive oil
- salt, ground pepper

For the dough (makes generous
1 lb/500 g linguine)

- 3 cups (400 g) all-purpose flour
- 4 large eggs
- 2 tbsp (30 ml) squid ink
- ¹/₃ cup (80 ml) olive oil
- 2 tsp (12 g) salt

》 Make the linguine dough as described in the basic recipe instructions for fresh pasta (see p. 20, § 1 and 2), mixing in the squid ink at the end.

》 When the dough has rested, roll it out on the work surface and make the linguine (strips approximately ¹/₁₀ inch/2–3 mm wide). Leave to dry for 2–3 hours.

》 Wash the squid thoroughly under cold water (keep them whole) and drain in a sieve.

》 Blanch the tomatoes in a pan of boiling water for 20 seconds and rinse under cold water. Remove the skins and seeds and chop them roughly.

》 Peel and chop the onion and garlic. Peel and finely dice the carrot and celery.

》 In a frying pan, brown the onion and garlic in 3 tablespoons of oil for 5 minutes on medium heat. Add the celery and carrot, stir well, and cook for 3 minutes. Add the squid and lightly brown them. Season with salt and pepper. Pour in the wine and squid ink. Cover the pan and simmer for 30 minutes on medium heat.

》 Remove the cover, reduce the heat, and cook for another 20 minutes or so, stirring frequently until the sauce has thickened. Keep it hot.

》 Cook the linguine in plenty of boiling salted water for 4–6 minutes. Drain and stir the remaining olive oil through the pasta in a bowl. Season with salt and pepper.

》 Serve the pasta in shallow bowls with the squid and ink sauce.

TAGLIATELLE WITH OYSTER MUSHROOMS AND DUCK BREAST

PREPARATION: **40 minutes + 4–5 hours drying time for the dough and tagliatelle**

COOKING THE PASTA:
4–5 minutes

INGREDIENTS

Serves 6

- 9 oz (250 g) smoked duck breast, sliced
- generous 1 lb (500 g) oyster mushrooms
- ¾ cup (100 g) pine nuts
- 3 shallots
- 1 bunch chervil
- $1/3$ cup (80 g) butter
- salt, ground pepper

For the dough (makes generous 1 lb/500 g tagliatelle)

- 3 cups (400 g) all-purpose flour
- 4 large eggs
- 2 tbsp poppy seeds
- $1/3$ cup (80 ml) olive oil
- 2 tsp (12 g) salt

≫ Make the tagliatelle dough as described in the basic recipe instructions for fresh pasta (see p. 20, § 1 and 2), mixing in the poppy seeds along with the oil.

≫ When the dough has rested, roll it out on the work surface and cut it into strips measuring approximately $1/5$ inch (5 mm) wide. Leave to dry for 2–3 hours.

≫ Clean the mushrooms and chop them finely.

≫ Chop the chervil. Remove the fat from the duck breasts.

≫ Peel and chop the shallots. Brown them in a frying pan with half the butter for 3 minutes on medium heat. Add the mushrooms and season with salt and pepper. Cook for 8–10 minutes on medium heat, stirring frequently.

≫ Add the pine nuts to the pan and brown for 2 minutes. Add the remaining butter, the chervil, and sliced duck. Stir well on high heat for 1 minute and then turn off the heat. Keep it hot.

≫ Cook the tagliatelle in plenty of boiling salted water for 4–5 minutes.

≫ Drain and transfer the pasta to a large dish. Add the contents of the frying pan and stir all the ingredients together well. Serve immediately.

TIP

In season, replace the oyster mushrooms in this recipe with edible wild mushrooms, such as chanterelles or morels.

LASAGNE WITH PARMESAN

**PREPARATION: 45 minutes
+ 4–5 hours drying time for the
dough and lasagne**

OVEN COOKING TIME:
45 minutes

INGREDIENTS

Serves 6

- 1¾ lb (800 g) ground beef
- ¾ lb (350 g) peeled, chopped
  tomatoes (canned)
- 1 carrot
- 1 onion
- ²/₃ cup (150 ml) white wine
- 3 tbsp olive oil + some for the dish
- salt, ground pepper

For the dough (makes generous
1 lb/500 g lasagne)

- 3 cups (400 g) all-purpose flour
- 4 large eggs
- ¹/₃ cup (80 ml) olive oil
- 2 tsp (12 g) salt

For the béchamel sauce

- 3 tbsp (30 g) all-purpose flour
- 2 cups (500 ml) milk
- generous 1 cup (120 g) grated
  Parmesan
- 2 pinches nutmeg
- 2 tbsp (30 g) butter
- salt, ground pepper

⟩ Make the lasagne dough as described in the basic recipe instructions for fresh pasta (see p. 20, § 1 and 2).

⟩ When the dough has rested, roll it out on the work surface (not too thinly) and cut it into strips measuring approximately 6 x 4 inches (15 x 10 cm). Leave to dry for 2–3 hours.

⟩ Peel and chop the onion. Peel and finely dice the carrot. Brown the onion and carrot in a frying pan in the olive oil for 2 minutes on medium heat. Add the ground beef and sear for 5 minutes on high heat. Season with salt and pepper. Pour in the wine and reduce for 5 minutes. Add the tomatoes and simmer for 30 minutes on medium heat.

⟩ Meanwhile, prepare the béchamel sauce. Melt the butter in a pan, add the flour, and cook for 3 minutes, beating constantly with a whisk to make a roux. Pour in the milk, season with the nutmeg and a pinch of salt and pepper, and cook for 5 minutes on medium heat until it thickens, stirring frequently.

❯ Pre-heat the oven to 210 °C (410 °F).

❯ Line a large, greased gratin dish with lasagne sheets. Spread one third of the meat mixture over the lasagne and cover with a little béchamel sauce. Repeat the process twice more. Finish with a layer of lasagne and coat with the béchamel sauce. Sprinkle the Parmesan on top.

❯ Bake in the oven for 45 minutes. Serve immediately with a green salad.

POPPY SEED TAGLIATELLE WITH BLACK PEPPER CREAM, CHIPOLATAS, AND PECORINO

PREPARATION: **45 minutes + 4 hours drying time for the dough and tagliatelle**

COOKING THE PASTA: **5–6 minutes**

INGREDIENTS

Serves 6

- 9 herb chipolatas
- 1 $^1/_3$ cups (150 g) Pecorino cheese
- 1 bunch chervil
- ½ bunch chives
- 1 $^2/_3$ cups (400 ml) light cream
- 2½ tbsp (40 g butter)
- 1 tbsp oil
- scant 2 tbsp freshly ground black pepper

For the dough (makes generous 1 lb/500 g tagliatelle)

- 3 cups (400 g) all-purpose flour
- 4 large eggs
- 2 tbsp (15 g) poppy seeds
- $^1/_3$ cup (80 ml) olive oil
- 2 tsp (12 g) salt

> Make the tagliatelle dough as described in the basic recipe instructions for fresh pasta (see p. 20, § 1 and 2), mixing in the poppy seeds together with the oil.

> When the dough has rested, roll it out on the work surface and cut into strips measuring approximately $^1/_5$ inch (5 mm) wide. Leave to dry for 2 hours.

> Boil the cream in a pan to reduce it by one quarter. Add the butter and pepper. Whizz the sauce with a hand blender until smooth and keep it hot.

> Chop the herbs. Make Pecorino shavings using a vegetable peeler. Set aside.

> In a frying pan, cook the sausages in the oil for 8–10 minutes on medium heat.

> Meanwhile, cook the tagliatelle in plenty of boiling salted water for 5–6 minutes.

> Drain the pasta and tip into a bowl. Stir through the hot pepper sauce.

> Spoon the pasta onto the plates. Add the sausages, chopped into pieces. Sprinkle with Pecorino shavings and chopped herbs. Serve immediately.

ORECCHIETTE SALAD WITH EGG AND HERBS

PREPARATION: 40 minutes + 8 hours drying time for the dough and orecchiette; 1 hour in refrigerator for the salad

COOKING THE PASTA:
10 minutes

INGREDIENTS

Serves 6

- 8 eggs
- 1 large bunch chervil
- 4 sprigs tarragon
- generous 1 tsp mustard
- 3 tbsp walnut vinegar
- 7 tbsp (100 ml) olive oil
- salt, ground pepper

For the dough (makes generous 1 lb/500 g orecchiette)

- 3 cups (400 g) all-purpose flour
- 4 large eggs
- $1/3$ cup (80 ml) olive oil
- 2 tsp (12 g) salt

≫ Make the orecchiette dough as described in the basic recipe instructions for fresh pasta (see p. 20, § 1 and 2).

≫ When the dough has rested, roll it out on the work surface. Make the orecchiette (as shown on p. 17). Leave to dry flat on wax paper.

≫ Cook the orecchiette for 10 minutes in plenty of boiling salted water. Drain in a sieve and rinse under cold water.

≫ Chop the herbs. Hard-cook the eggs for 10 minutes in a pan of boiling water. Rinse under cold water, remove the shells, and chop them up.

≫ In a bowl, mix the mustard, vinegar, and some salt and pepper together with 2 tablespoons of water. Whisk in the olive oil. Add the herbs, chopped eggs, and cold drained pasta. Chill the salad for at least 1 hour.

Pep the sauce up with wholegrain or flavored mustard.

TURMERIC FETTUCCINE WITH VEAL AND ZUCCHINI

PREPARATION: **1 hour**
+ 5 hours drying time for the
dough and fettuccine

COOKING THE PASTA:
3–4 minutes

INGREDIENTS

Serves 6

- 6 veal escalopes
- 6 very ripe tomatoes
- 3 medium zucchini
- 2 shallots
- 2 cloves garlic
- 10 sage leaves
- 1¼ cups (300 ml) vegetable stock
- 7 tbsp (100 ml) olive oil
- salt, ground pepper

For the dough (makes generous
1 lb/500 g fettuccine)

- 3 cups (400 g) all-purpose flour
- 4 large eggs
- 1 tsp turmeric
- ¹/₃ cup (80 ml) olive oil
- 2 tsp (12 g) salt

≫ Make the fettuccine dough as described in the basic recipe instructions for fresh pasta (see p. 20, § 1 and 2), mixing in the turmeric together with the oil.

≫ When the dough has rested, roll it out on the work surface and cut it into fettuccine strips (long, wide tagliatelle). Leave to dry for at least 3 hours.

≫ Blanch the tomatoes in boiling water for 30 seconds and rinse under cold water. Peel, de-seed, and chop the tomatoes.

≫ Peel and chop the shallots and garlic. Sweat the shallots and garlic in a pan with half the olive oil for 3 minutes on medium heat. Add the chopped tomatoes, stock, and some salt and pepper. Cook for 20 minutes on medium heat. Whizz the mixture with a hand blender until it is smooth and slightly runny. Add the chopped sage. Keep the sauce hot.

≫ Slice the escalopes. Wash the zucchini and cut into thin strips. In a large frying pan, sear the veal escalopes with the remaining oil for 2 minutes on each side. Season with salt and pepper. Add the zucchini strips and stir fry for 3–4 minutes on high heat. Keep it hot.

≫ Cook the fettuccine in plenty of boiling salted water for 3–4 minutes. Drain and spoon into shallow bowls.

≫ Arrange the meat and zucchini on top of the pasta. Pour on the tomato sauce and serve immediately.

RAVIOLI

Ravioli with creamy anchovy and red pepper

PREPARATION: 50 minutes + 2 hours drying time for the dough + 2 hours in refrigerator

COOKING THE RAVIOLI:
3–4 minutes

INGREDIENTS

Serves 6

- 2 red bell peppers
- 2 tbsp (30 g) anchovy paste
- 3 tbsp (45 ml) light cream
- 1 small bunch lemon thyme
- 1 cup (250 ml) fish stock
- 7 tbsp (100 ml) olive oil
- salt, ground pepper

For the dough (makes generous 1 lb/500 g ravioli)

- 3 cups (400 g) all-purpose flour
- 4 large eggs
- 1/3 cup (80 ml) olive oil
- 2 tsp (12 g) salt

> Make the ravioli dough as described in the basic recipe instructions for fresh pasta (see p. 20, § 1 and 2).

> Meanwhile, pre-heat the oven to 180 °C (350 °F). Wrap the peppers separately in pieces of aluminum foil and bake for 30–35 minutes. Take them out of the oven and leave to cool down in the foil. Remove the skin, cut off the stems, and remove the seeds. Rinse under cold water and drain. Chop the peppers roughly and stir in the anchovy paste and light cream.

> When the dough has rested, roll it out on the work surface into fairly wide strips. Make the ravioli (as shown on p. 18), stuffing them with scant 1 teaspoon of the anchovy and pepper mixture. Chill for 2 hours.

> In a pan, boil the fish stock rapidly with the thyme sprigs and a little salt and pepper until reduced in volume by one third. Remove from the heat and add the olive oil. Strain the sauce and whizz it with a hand blender until smooth. Keep it hot.

> Just before you are ready to serve, simmer the ravioli gently for 3–4 minutes in plenty of boiling salted water.

> Drain the ravioli and spoon them onto the plates. Pour on the sauce and serve immediately.

GOAT CHEESE, PINE NUT, AND BASIL PARCELS

PREPARATION: 45 minutes + 2 hours drying time for the dough + 2 hours in refrigerator

COOKING THE RAVIOLI: 4–5 minutes

INGREDIENTS

Serves 6

- 10 oz (280 g) fresh goat cheese
- 9 tbsp (75 g) pine nuts
- 20 large basil leaves
- 1 ²/₃ cups (400 ml) vegetable stock
- 1 tbsp thick crème fraîche
- 2½ tbsp (40 g) butter
- salt, ground pepper

For the dough (makes generous 1 lb/500 g ravioli)

- 3 cups (400 g) all-purpose flour
- 4 large eggs
- ¹/₃ cup (80 ml) olive oil
- 2 tsp (12 g) salt

≫ Make the ravioli dough as described in the basic recipe instructions for fresh pasta (see p. 20, § 1 and 2).

≫ While the dough is resting, dry-roast the pine nuts in a pan before turning them onto a paper towel. Chop half the basil and put in a bowl along with the goat cheese, pine nuts, and some salt and pepper. Mash all the ingredients together with a fork. Put to one side.

≫ When the dough has rested, roll it into fairly wide strips. Cut out 30 circles measuring just over 3 inches (8 cm) in diameter. Place a spoonful of the cheese mixture in the middle of each circle, then gather the edges together, closing them up like a pouch—press the edges together firmly to seal them. Chill for 2 hours.

≫ In a pan, boil the vegetable stock rapidly for 5 minutes, adding a little salt and pepper. Add the crème fraîche and chopped butter. Boil for another 5 minutes. Remove the pan from the heat and mix in the rest of the basil. Whizz with a hand blender until smooth. Keep it hot.

≫ Just before you are ready to serve, simmer the ravioli for 4–5 minutes in plenty of salted water.

≫ Drain the ravioli and spoon into shallow dishes. Pour on the sauce and serve immediately.

Ravioli with smoked sausage and cider

PREPARATION: **1 hour**
+ 2 hours in refrigerator

COOKING THE RAVIOLI:
4–5 minutes

INGREDIENTS

Serves 6

- generous 1 lb (500 g) ready-made ravioli sheets (from the fresh food section)
- ¾ lb (350 g) smoked sausage
- 4 oz (120 g) Camembert
- 1 Golden Delicious apple
- generous 1 tbsp caraway seeds
- 1 tbsp veal or beef stock powder
- 2½ cups (600 ml) cider
- $^1/_3$ cup (80 g) butter
- salt, ground pepper

≫ Remove the sausage skin and dice the meat finely.

≫ Peel the apple and dice finely. Cook the apple in a frying pan with 2 tablespoons of butter for 8–10 minutes on medium heat. Add the chopped sausage and brown for 4–5 minutes. Season with salt and pepper and add the caraway seeds. Leave to cool down completely.

≫ Chop the Camembert into small pieces and add to the frying pan.

≫ Cut the ravioli sheets into 48 squares. Spoon a little of the sausage mix in the middle of 24 of the squares. Moisten the sides with a little water and cover with the remaining 24 squares, pressing down the edges to seal the ravioli completely. Chill for 2 hours.

≫ Stir the stock powder into the cider and reduce for 10–15 minutes in a frying pan on medium heat, until it thickens. Whip in the cold chopped butter and season with salt and pepper. Keep the sauce hot.

≫ Cook the ravioli for 4–5 minutes in plenty of boiling salted water. Drain and add them to the cider sauce. Simmer for 2 minutes. Serve immediately.

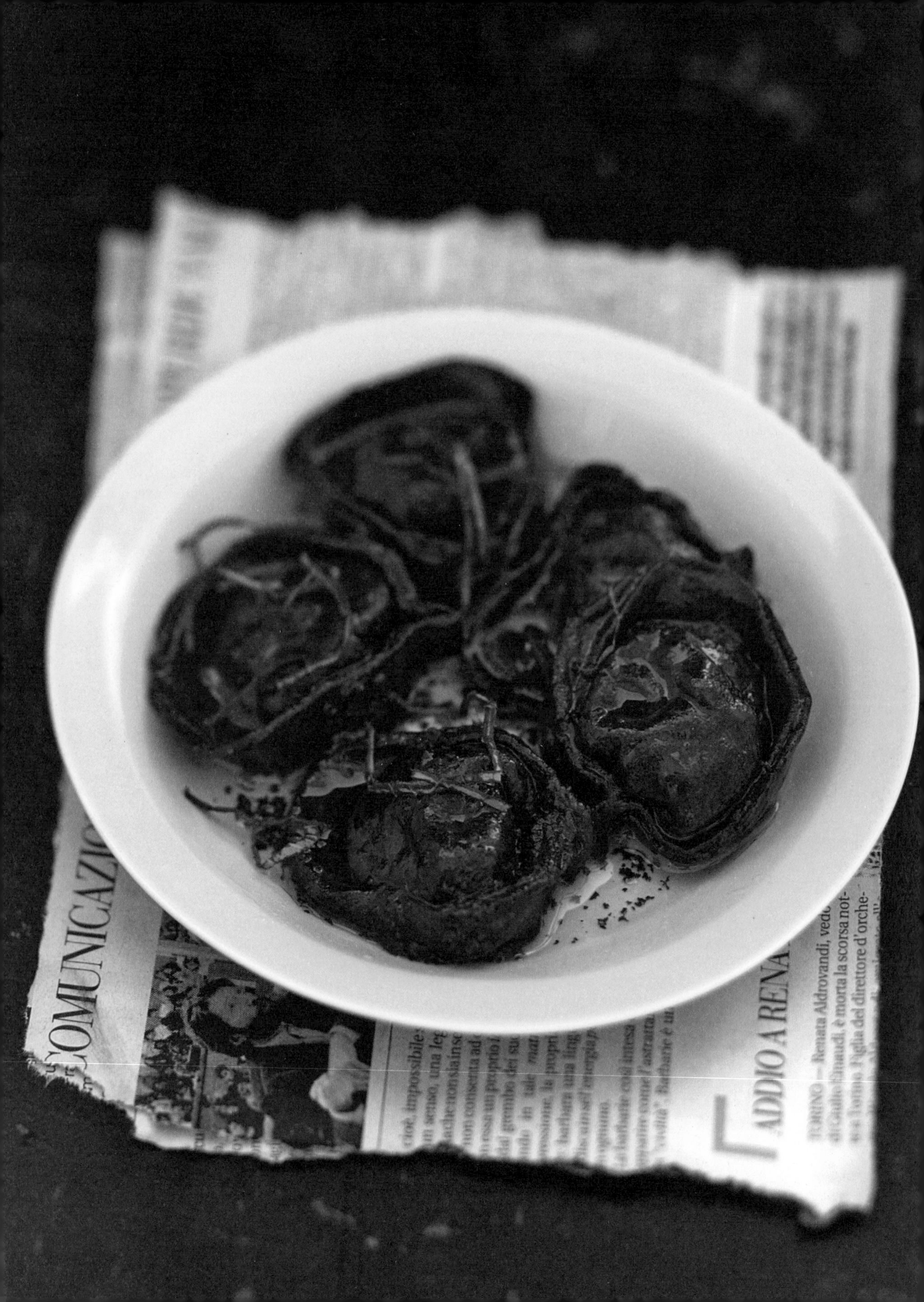
COMUNICAZI
ADDIO A RENA
TORINO — Renata Aldrovandi, vedo

PREPARATION: **1 hour**
+ 2 hours drying time for the dough
+ 2 hours in refrigerator

COOKING THE TORTELLI:
5 minutes

BLACK TORTELLI WITH SMOKED SALMON AND TAPENADE

INGREDIENTS

Serves 6

- 7 oz (200 g) smoked salmon
- 2 oz (60 g) tapenade
- 6½ oz (180 g) full-fat soft cream cheese
- ^{2}/$_3$ cup (150 ml) olive oil
- 10 basil leaves
- salt, ground pepper

For the dough (makes generous 1 lb/500 g tortelli)

- 3 cups (400 g) all-purpose flour
- 4 large eggs
- 2 tbsp (30 ml) squid ink
- ^{1}/$_3$ cup (80 ml) olive oil
- 1½ tsp (8 g) salt

≫ Make the tortelli dough as described in the basic recipe instructions for fresh pasta (see p. 20, § 1 and 2), mixing in the squid ink at the end.

≫ While the dough is resting, chop the smoked salmon. Mix the salmon with the cream cheese in a bowl along with 1½ ounces (40 g) of tapenade, 2 tablespoons of olive oil, and some pepper (no salt). Set to one side.

≫ When the dough has rested, roll it into fairly wide strips. Cut out 30–36 circles measuring just over 3 inches (8 cm) in diameter. Put a spoonful of the salmon mix on each piece of dough and shape into tortelli (as shown on p. 19). Chill for at least 2 hours.

≫ Stir together the rest of the olive oil and tapenade. Add the chopped basil leaves, some pepper, and a pinch of salt.

≫ Just before you are ready to serve, simmer the tortelli for 4–5 minutes in plenty of salted water and drain them.

≫ Spoon the tortelli onto the plates and coat with the tapenade oil. Serve immediately.

RAVIOLI WITH MINTED PEAS

**PREPARATION: 45 minutes
+ 2 hours drying time for the
dough + 2 hours in refrigerator**

COOKING THE RAVIOLI:
4—5 minutes

INGREDIENTS

Serves 6

- 7 oz (200 g) shelled, fresh young
  peas
- 1 bunch fresh mint
- 7 oz (200 g) full-fat soft cream
  cheese
- 1 $^2/_3$ cups (400 ml) vegetable stock
- $^1/_3$ cup (80 g) butter
- salt, ground pepper

**For the dough (makes generous
1 lb/500 g ravioli)**

- 3 cups (400 g) all-purpose flour
- 4 large eggs
- $^1/_3$ cup (80 ml) olive oil
- 2 tsp (12 g) salt

> Make the ravioli dough as described in the basic recipe instructions for fresh pasta (see p. 20, § 1 and 2).

> While the dough is resting, cook the peas in boiling salted water for 10—12 minutes. Drain and whizz the peas right away with 1½ tablespoons (20 g) of the butter to make a silky smooth purée. Leave to cool down. Stir in the cream cheese and a few finely chopped mint leaves. Season with salt and pepper.

> When the dough has rested, roll it into fairly wide strips. Cut out 30—36 circles measuring just over 3 inches (8cm) in diameter. Put a spoonful of the pea mixture on one side of each circle and fold over the other side to form semi-circles. Press the edges together firmly to seal. Chill the ravioli for at least 2 hours.

> Boil the vegetable stock for 5 minutes in a pan. Season with salt and pepper, add the rest of the butter, and boil rapidly for a further 5 minutes. Remove from the heat and add the remaining chopped mint leaves. Whizz the sauce with a hand blender and keep it hot.

> Just before you are ready to serve, simmer the ravioli for 4—5 minutes in plenty of salted water.

> Drain the ravioli and spoon them onto the plates. Pour on the sauce and serve immediately.

TORTELLI WITH HAM, RICOTTA, AND WALNUT CREAM

PREPARATION: **1 hour + 2 hours drying time for the dough + 2 hours in refrigerator**

COOKING THE TORTELLI: **3 minutes**

INGREDIENTS

Serves 6

- 5 slices Bayonne (or other dried cured) ham
- ¾ lb (350 g) ricotta cheese
- 1¼ cups (150 g) chopped walnuts
- ¼ cup (30 g) freshly grated Parmesan
- 1 tbsp chopped chervil
- scant 1 tbsp Espelette pepper
- 1 $^2/_3$ cups (400 ml) light cream
- 3 tbsp olive oil
- 1 tbsp sunflower oil
- salt, ground pepper

For the dough (makes generous 1 lb/500 g tortelli)

- 3 cups (400 g) all-purpose flour
- 4 large eggs
- ½ tsp turmeric
- $^1/_3$ cup (80 ml) olive oil
- 2 tsp (12 g) salt

≫ Make the tortelli dough as described in the basic recipe instructions for fresh pasta (see p. 20, § 1 and 2).

≫ While the dough is resting, cut the ham into very thin strips. Brown the ham in a frying pan in the sunflower oil for 2–3 minutes on high heat. Transfer to a plate lined with paper towel.

≫ In a bowl, mix together the ricotta, Espelette pepper, olive oil, ham strips, and a pinch of salt.

≫ When the dough has rested, roll it out on the work surface into fairly wide strips. Cut out 30–36 circles measuring just over 3 inches (8 cm) in diameter. Place a spoonful of the ricotta mixture in the center of each piece of dough and shape them into tortelli (as shown on p. 19). Chill for at least 2 hours.

≫ Boil the cream in a pan for 5 minutes. Remove from the heat and add 3½ ounces (100 g) of chopped walnuts, the Parmesan, and some salt and pepper. Whizz the sauce with a hand blender. Keep it hot.

≫ Just before you are ready to serve, simmer the tortelli for 3 minutes in plenty of boiling salted water and drain.

≫ Spoon the tortelli onto the plates. Pour on the sauce and sprinkle with the remaining chopped walnuts and the chervil.

RAVIOLI WITH BRAISED OXTAIL

PREPARATION: **4 hours + 2 hours drying time for the dough + 2 hours in refrigerator**

COOKING THE RAVIOLI:
4–5 minutes

INGREDIENTS

Serves 6

- 3¼ lb (1.5 kg) oxtail, cut into pieces
- 2 carrots, peeled and chopped
- 1 onion, peeled and chopped
- 1 bouquet garni
- 1 bunch fresh thyme
- 2 cups (500 ml) red wine
- 2 tbsp (30 g) butter
- 3 tbsp sunflower oil
- salt, ground pepper

For the dough (makes generous 1 lb/500 g ravioli)

- 3 cups (400 g) all-purpose flour
- 4 large eggs
- ¹/₃ cup (80 ml) olive oil
- 2 tsp (12 g) salt

≫ In a casserole, sear the oxtail pieces all over in the very hot oil for 5 minutes. Add the carrots and onion and cook for 3 minutes, stirring all the time. Pour in the wine and add enough water to cover the meat. Add the bouquet garni and a pinch of salt and pepper. Cover the casserole and simmer very gently for 3 hours, adding a little water if required.

≫ Meanwhile, make the ravioli dough as described in the basic recipe instructions for fresh pasta (see p. 20, § 1 and 2).

≫ While the dough is resting, drain the oxtail pieces and leave them to cool down a bit (reserving the cooking stock). Carefully remove all the meat from the bones. Chop the meat roughly and add a few sprigs of thyme.

≫ When the dough has rested, roll it into fairly wide strips. Cut out 30–36 circles (or squares) measuring approximately 4 inches (10 cm) in diameter. Put a spoonful of the oxtail meat in the middle of 18 circles (or squares), moisten the edges with a little water, and cover with the remaining dough shapes. Press the edges together firmly to seal the ravioli. Chill for at least 2 hours.

≫ Strain the cooking stock and reduce it slightly in a pan with the rest of the thyme. Whisk in the cold chopped butter. Keep it hot.

≫ Just before you are ready to serve, simmer the ravioli for 4–5 minutes in plenty of boiling salted water. Drain and then spoon the ravioli into shallow bowls. Pour on the thyme sauce. Serve immediately.

Jumbo ravioli with lobster, ginger, coconut, and cilantro

**PREPARATION: 1 hour
+ 2 hours drying time for the
dough + 2 hours in refrigerator**

**COOKING THE RAVIOLI:
3–4 minutes**

INGREDIENTS

Serves 6

- 1 cooked lobster, weighing
  1¼–1¾ lb (600–800 g)
- 1 onion
- 1 bunch cilantro, chopped
- 1¼ cups (300 ml) coconut milk
- generous ¾ cup (200 ml) fish stock
- 1 tbsp (14 g) fresh ginger, peeled
  and chopped
- 3½ tbsp (50 g) butter
- 7 tbsp (100 ml) olive oil
- salt, ground pepper

**For the dough (makes generous
1 lb/500 g ravioli)**

- 3 cups (400 g) all-purpose flour
- 4 large eggs
- 1 tsp turmeric
- ¹/₃ cup (80 ml) olive oil
- 2 tsp (12 g) salt

≫ Make the ravioli dough as described in the basic recipe instructions for fresh pasta (see p. 20, § 1 and 2), incorporating the turmeric with the oil.

≫ While the dough is resting, remove all the lobster shell and dice the meat finely. Peel and chop the onion. Sweat it in a frying pan with half the olive oil for 5 minutes on medium heat. Add the lobster meat, half the ginger and cilantro, and some salt and pepper. Mix well and cook for 2 minutes on medium heat. Leave to cool.

≫ When the dough has rested, roll it into fairly wide 6 inch (15 cm) strips on the work surface, not too thinly. Cut out 12 circles measuring 5–5½ inches (12–14 cm) in diameter.

≫ Divide the lobster filling between 6 dough circles. Moisten round the edges with a little water and cover with the other 6 rounds. Press the edges down firmly to seal the ravioli. Chill on a plate dusted with flour for 2 hours.

≫ In a pan, add the coconut milk and seasoning to the fish stock and reduce by one quarter. Remove from the heat, add the cold chopped butter, along with the remaining oil, ginger, and cilantro. Whizz the sauce with a hand blender until silky smooth. Keep it hot.

≫ Just before you are ready to serve, simmer the ravioli for 3–4 minutes in plenty of boiling salted water. Drain and place 1 jumbo ravioli in each pasta bowl. Whizz the hot sauce again and pour it over the ravioli. Serve immediately.

PREPARATION: **45 minutes**
+ 2 hours resting time
+ 2 hours in refrigerator

OVEN COOKING TIME: **20—25 minutes**

BAKED PARMESAN GNOCCHI

INGREDIENTS

Serves 6

- 2¼ lb (1 kg) potatoes, firm texture
- generous 1 $^1/_3$—1 $^2/_3$ cups
  (200–230 g) all-purpose flour
  + 2 or 3 tbsp
- 1 egg
- salt, ground pepper

For the béchamel sauce

- 5 tbsp (40 g) all-purpose flour
- 2½ cups (600 ml) milk
- 1 $^1/_3$ cups (150 g) grated Parmesan
- nutmeg
- 2½ tbsp (40 g) butter + 1½ tbsp
  (20 g) to grease the dish
- salt, ground pepper

> Wash the potatoes and cook for 20—25 minutes in a pan containing boiling salted water. Drain and then peel the potatoes while still warm. Press the potato through a potato ricer into a bowl. Add generous 1 $^1/_3$—1 $^2/_3$ cups (200–230 g) flour (depending on the type of potatoes you use), the egg, and some salt and pepper. Mix together well until you have a dry dough.

> When the dough has rested, roll it into thin sausage shapes approximately ½ inch (1.5 cm) in diameter. Cut into ¾ inch (2 cm) sections and press down lightly with a fork. Put them on a floured tray and chill in the refrigerator for 2 hours.

> To make the béchamel sauce, first melt the butter in a pan, then add the flour, and cook for 3 minutes, stirring all the time until you have a smooth, pale roux. Add the cold milk and 2 pinches of nutmeg, and season with salt and pepper. Bring to a boil and cook for 3—4 minutes on medium heat, whisking continuously—the sauce should be fairly thin. Remove from the heat and stir in half the Parmesan.

> Pre-heat the oven to 180 °C (350 °F).

» Carefully drop the gnocchi into a pan with plenty of boiling salted water—they are cooked when they rise to the surface. Drain the gnocchi and transfer them to a buttered gratin dish.

» Smother the gnocchi with the béchamel sauce, smooth over the surface, and sprinkle with Parmesan.

» Bake for 20—25 minutes. Serve with salad or as an accompaniment to white meat or poultry.

Ravioli with sesame, langoustines, basil, and lardo

PREPARATION: **45 minutes + 2 hours drying time for the dough + 2 hours in refrigerator**

COOKING THE RAVIOLI: **3—4 minutes**

INGREDIENTS

Serves 6

- 24 extra large langoustines
- 24 thin slices *lardo di Collonnata* (Tuscan cured, spiced pork fat)
- 24 large basil leaves + 15 for the sauce
- ²/₃ cup (150 ml) olive oil
- salt, ground pepper

For the dough (makes generous 1 lb/500 g ravioli)

- 3 cups (400 g) all-purpose flour
- 4 large eggs
- 5 tbsp (50 g) black sesame seeds
- ¹/₃ cup (80 ml) olive oil
- 2 tsp (12 g) salt

≫ Make the ravioli dough as described in the basic recipe instructions for fresh pasta (see p. 20, § 1 and 2), mixing in the sesame seeds together with the oil.

≫ While the dough is resting, remove the langoustine shells (including the heads) making sure you keep the tails whole. Make a slit down the back of the tails and remove the black veins.

≫ In a frying pan, sear the langoustines in 2 tablespoons of olive oil for 1—2 minutes. Season with salt and pepper. Transfer them onto paper towels and leave to cool down.

≫ When the dough has rested, roll it out on the work surface into fairly wide strips. Cut out 24 circles measuring approximately 4 inches (10 cm) in diameter.

≫ Wrap 1 slice *lardo di Collonnata* and 1 basil leaf around each langoustine tail. Place the langoustines on the pasta rounds and close them over into semi-circles, taking care to seal them. Chill for 2 hours.

≫ Pour the rest of the oil into a bowl with the 15 remaining basil leaves and some salt and pepper. Whizz with a hand blender to make basil oil.

≫ Just before you are ready to serve, simmer the ravioli for 3—4 minutes in plenty of boiling salted water. Drain them.

≫ Spoon the ravioli onto the plates. Drizzle all over with basil oil and serve immediately.

RAVIOLI CRACKERS, MASCARPONE, AND BERRY COMPOTE

PREPARATION: **30 minutes**

COOKING THE CRACKERS:
2–3 minutes

INGREDIENTS

Serves 6

- 12 sheets dried lasagne
- scant 2½ cups (600 g) mascarpone
- generous 1 lb (500 g) mixed berries, fresh or frozen (e.g. raspberries, blueberries, blackcurrants)
- 1 vanilla pod
- 3 tbsp barley malt syrup
- 1 quart (1 liter) oil for deep-frying
- scant 1 cup (100 g) powdered (icing) sugar
- ½ cup (100 g) superfine sugar

≫ Split open the vanilla pod lengthwise and scrape out the seeds with the tip of a knife. Mix the vanilla seeds into the mascarpone and fold in the powdered sugar. Chill the mixture.

≫ Rinse the berries briefly in a sieve under cold running water.

≫ In a pan, heat the barley malt syrup with 7 tablespoons of superfine sugar for 3 minutes on high heat. Add the berries and cook on high heat for 4–5 minutes, stirring gently until they thicken to the consistency of a compote. Keep the mixture at room temperature.

≫ Cook the lasagne sheets for 2 minutes in plenty of boiling water (unsalted). Drain in a sieve and rinse under cold water. Lay the lasagne sheets out immediately on a clean cloth to dry, then place them on the work surface. Cut out the crackers using the shape of pastry cutter you prefer.

≫ Heat the oil in a pan and deep-fry the crackers in small batches for a few seconds at a time. Drain on paper towels and dust with the remaining superfine sugar.

≫ Spoon the mascarpone into small bowls and top with the berry compote. Serve with the crunchy crackers.

RAVIOLI WITH LEMON RICOTTA

PREPARATION: **50 minutes + 2 hours drying time for the dough + 2 hours in refrigerator**

COOKING THE RAVIOLI: 3–4 minutes

INGREDIENTS

Serves 6

- scant 1 cup (220 g) ricotta
- peel of 1 preserved lemon
- ¾ cup (140 g) superfine sugar
- 2 lemons
- 3 tbsp lemon syrup
- 7 tbsp (100 ml) limoncello

For the dough (makes generous 1 lb/500 g ravioli)

- 3 cups (400 g) all-purpose flour
- 4 large eggs
- juice and zest of 1 lemon
- ¼–¹⁄₃ cup (60–80 ml) groundnut oil
- 1½ tbsp (20 g) superfine sugar

❯ Make the ravioli dough as described in the basic recipe instructions for fresh pasta (see p. 20, § 1 and 2), replacing the salt with the sugar and incorporating the lemon zest and juice along with the oil.

❯ While the dough is resting, dice the preserved lemon peel very finely. Squeeze the juice of 1 lemon and zest it.

❯ In a bowl, mix together the ricotta, 7 tablespoons of sugar, the preserved lemon, and the lemon zest and juice.

❯ When the dough has rested, roll it into fairly wide strips on the work surface. Cut the dough into 36 rectangles measuring approximately 2½ x 4 inches (6 x 10 cm). Make the ravioli (as shown on p. 18) and fill them with the ricotta mixture. Chill for 2 hours.

❯ Squeeze the juice from the other lemon and zest it. In a large pan, boil the limoncello, lemon juice, lemon zest, lemon syrup, and the remaining sugar for 8–10 minutes on medium heat until quite thick and syrupy. Leave to cool.

❯ Just before you are ready to serve, simmer the ravioli for 3–4 minutes in plenty of boiling water and then drain them.

❯ Spoon the ravioli onto the plates and drizzle with the limoncello syrup.

CHOCOLATE RAVIOLI

PREPARATION: **50 minutes + 2 hours drying time for the dough + 2 hours in refrigerator**

COOKING THE RAVIOLI:

3–4 minutes

INGREDIENTS

Serves 6

For the garnish and sauce

- 10 tbsp (200 g) chocolate hazelnut spread
- 6½ oz (180 g) milk chocolate
- ²/₃ cup (80 g) chopped hazelnuts
- 7 tbsp (100 ml) milk
- 7 tbsp (100 ml) light cream
- ¹/₃ cup (60 g) superfine sugar

For the dough (makes generous 1 lb/500 g ravioli)

- 2¾ cups (360 g) all-purpose flour
- 4 large eggs
- 7 tbsp (50 g) unsweetened cocoa
- ¼–¹/₃ cup (60–80 ml) groundnut oil
- 1¼ tbsp (15 g) superfine sugar

≫ Make the ravioli dough as described in the basic recipe instructions for fresh pasta (see p. 20, § 1 and 2), replacing the salt with the sugar and incorporating the cocoa with the oil.

≫ When the dough has rested, roll it out on the work surface into fairly wide strips. Cut out 48 circles measuring approximately 2½ inches (6–7 cm) in diameter.

≫ Put scant 1 teaspoon of chocolate nut spread in the middle of 24 dough circles, moisten the edges with a little water, and cover with the remaining dough rounds, pressing firmly all round the edges to seal the ravioli. Chill for 2 hours.

≫ Dry-roast the hazelnuts for 2 minutes in a frying pan.

≫ Chop up the chocolate with a knife. Bring the milk and cream to a boil in a pan. Remove from the heat, add the chocolate, and mix well until the sauce is silky smooth. Keep it warm in a double boiler.

≫ Just before you are ready to serve, boil up 1½ quarts (1.5 liters) of water in a pan with the sugar for 5 minutes. Lower the heat, drop the ravioli carefully into the simmering water, and allow to cook for 3–4 minutes. Drain them.

≫ Spoon the ravioli onto the plates, pour over the chocolate sauce, and sprinkle with the toasted hazelnuts. Serve immediately.

SAUCES

TOMATO SAUCE

Pre-heat the oven to 160 °C (320 °F). Blanch 2¼ pounds (1 kg) of very ripe tomatoes for 30 seconds in boiling water and then drain. Rinse under cold water, remove the skins and seeds, and chop roughly. Peel and chop 1 large onion and 3 garlic cloves, then sweat them in a casserole with 3 tablespoons of olive oil. Add the tomatoes, 1 sprig of thyme, 1 bay leaf, a few sprigs of rosemary, 1 tablespoon of sugar, generous ¾ cup (200 ml) of white wine, and a little salt and pepper. Stir well and bring to a boil. Put the casserole dish in the oven for 1 hour, stirring occasionally. Remove the thyme, bay leaf, and rosemary, then whizz the tomatoes with a hand blender. Strain the sauce and chill it. You can easily make large quantities of the sauce and freeze it, or store it in sterilized jars.

BOLOGNAISE SAUCE

Peel and finely dice 2 carrots. Peel and chop 1 onion. Brown the carrot and onion in a casserole dish in 3 tablespoons of olive oil for 5 minutes on medium heat. Add 2¾ pounds (1.2 kg) of ground beef, salt, and pepper, and sear for 5 minutes on high heat. Add 1¼ cups (300 ml) of passata, generous ¾ cup (200 ml) of veal or beef stock, 1 bay leaf, and 2 sprigs of thyme. Stir well and simmer for 30 minutes on medium heat. Remove the thyme and bay leaf.

CURRY SAUCE

Peel and chop 1 onion. Sweat in a pan with 3 tablespoons of olive oil for 5 minutes on medium heat. Add 1 tablespoon of Madras curry powder and brown for 2 minutes on medium heat, stirring all the time. Pour in 1¼ cups (300 ml) of vegetable stock and boil for 5 minutes. Add 1¼ cups (300 ml) of light cream, season with salt and pepper, and simmer for 10 minutes on medium heat. Whizz the sauce with a hand blender.

PESTO

In a frying pan, dry-roast 7 tablespoons of pine nuts for 2 minutes on medium heat. Leave to cool. Put them in a mini-grinder with 30 basil leaves, 4 garlic cloves (peeled and green shoots removed), ⅔ cup (150 ml) of olive oil, and some salt and pepper. Whizz for 1–2 minutes into a smooth paste. Transfer the pesto to a bowl and add generous ½ cup (60 g) of grated Parmesan.

GORGONZOLA SAUCE

Bring 1⅔ cups (400 ml) of light cream to a boil in a pan for 5 minutes to reduce it slightly. Add 2 cups (220 g) of chopped Gorgonzola cheese and season to taste with salt and pepper. Stir gently with a spatula on low heat until the cheese has melted. Keep it hot in a double boiler.

Tomato sauce

Pesto

Curry sauce

Bolognaise sauce

Gorgonzola sauce

CONVERSIONS

LIQUIDS

Metric	American measure	Imperial
5 ml	1 tsp	1 tsp
15 ml	1 tbsp	1 tbsp
35 ml	2½ tbsp	2½ tbsp
65 ml	¼ cup	2 fl oz
125 ml	½ cup	4½ fl oz
250 ml	1 cup	9 fl oz
500 ml	2 cups	17 fl oz
1 liter	4 cups	1 quart

SOLIDS

Metric	American measure	Imperial
30 g	1 oz	1 oz
55 g	2 oz	2 oz
115 g	4 oz	4 oz
170 g	6 oz	6 oz
225 g	8 oz	8 oz
454 g	1 lb	1 lb

OVEN TEMPERATURES

Temperature	° Celsius	° Fahrenheit	Gas mark
Very cool	140 °C	275 °F	1
Cool	150 °C	300 °F	2
Warm	160 °C	325 °F	3
Moderate	180 °C	350 °F	4
Fairly hot	190–200 °C	375–400 °F	5–6
Hot	220 °C	425 °F	7
Very hot	230–240 °C	450–475 °F	8–9

I am extremely grateful to Barbara, Aurélie, and Mathilde for entrusting me with another title in this series. My thanks also go to Pierre-Louis for his input—excellent, as ever! And to Kenwood for the use of the Kmix food processor for making the recipes, Mauviel for the frying pans and casserole dishes, and Smeg for the stovetop.

It is advisable not to serve dishes that contain raw eggs to very young children, pregnant women, elderly people, or to anyone weakened by serious illness. If in any doubt, consult your doctor. Be sure that all the eggs you use are as fresh as possible.

© Mango, Paris — 2012

Original Title: *Pasta! Lasagne, Ravioli et Cannelloni*

ISBN 978-23-17003-55-4

Editorial team: Barbara Sabatier, Aurélie Cazenave and Mathilde Croizeau

Graphic Design: Laurent Quellet

Production: Thierry Dubus and Marie Guibert

© for this English edition: h.f.ullmann publishing GmbH

Translation from French: Ann Drummond, in association with First Edition Translations Ltd, Cambridge, UK

Overall responsibility for production:
h.f.ullmann publishing GmbH, Potsdam, Germany

Printed in India, 2015

ISBN 978-3-8480-0758-5

10 9 8 7 6 5 4 3 2 1
X IX VIII VII VI V IV III II I

www.ullmann-publishing.com
newsletter@ullmann-publishing.com
facebook.com/ullmann.social

In this series: